The Devil Reads Derrida

Also by James K. A. Smith

The Fall of Interpretation
Speech and Theology
Introducing Radical Orthodoxy
Jacques Derrida: Live Theory
Who's Afraid of Postmodernism?
Desiring the Kingdom: Worship, Worldview, and Cultural Formation
The Hermeneutics of Charity (co-editor)
Radical Orthodoxy and the Reformed Tradition (co-editor)
Hermeneutics at the Crossroads (co-editor)
After Modernity? (editor)

THE DEVIL READS DERRIDA

and Other Essays on the University, the Church, Politics, and the Arts

JAMES K. A. SMITH

WILLIAM B. EERDMANS PUBLISHING COMPANY

GRAND RAPIDS, MICHIGAN / CAMBRIDGE, U.K.

Published 2009 by

WM. B. EERDMANS PUBLISHING CO.

2140 Oak Industrial Drive N.E., Grand Rapids, Michigan 49505 /

P.O. Box 163, Cambridge CB3 9PU U.K.

Printed in the United States of America

15 14 13 12 11 10 09   7 6 5 4 3 2 1

Library of Congress Cataloging-in-Publication Data

Smith, James K. A. 1970-
    The devil reads Derrida: and other essays on the university,
the church, politics, and the arts / James K. A. Smith.
    p.   cm.
   ~~ISBN 978-0-8028-6407-9 (pbk.: alk. paper)~~
    1. Christianity. I Title.
    BR50.S653   2009
    261 — dc22

                                          2009012122

www.eerdmans.com

For Richard Mouw,

who — like Good King Wenceslas — has gone before,
making tracks in which I could step,
though with footprints I could never hope to fill.

CONTENTS

ACKNOWLEDGMENTS

My thanks to editors and publishers for permission to reprint the essays collected here (the original publication information for each piece is indicated at the beginning of each chapter). I am particularly grateful to two magazines and their editors for providing a welcome venue for my writing in this genre. Scott Hoezee, Jim Bratt, and all the good folks at *Perspectives,* heir to the *Reformed Journal,* have carved out a unique niche within a generously construed Reformed tradition that takes not only the so-called life of the mind seriously, but also the workaday life that most people inhabit outside the rather surreal environment that is the academy. In a similar way, Gideon Strauss, Dan Postma, and the team at *Comment* magazine, published by the Work Research Foundation in Canada (now Cardus), have over just a few short years built a publication that is quite singular in its conjoining depth of analysis with breadth of audience. It has been (and continues to be) an honor and pleasure to be associated with these magazines, which, though not part of an East Coast elite culture, or even "mainstream" Christian publishing, can for that very reason speak to different publics in thoughtful, challenging, and provocative ways. Both of them deserve to be on more coffee tables than they are; I hope their readership continues to increase.

My thanks also to all the editors and publishers of magazines and periodicals in which the following essays first saw the light of publication, from flagship publications like *Christianity Today, Christian Century, Harvard Divinity Bulletin,* and *Books & Culture,* to newspapers such as the

Dubuque Telegraph Herald and the *Grand Rapids Press,* online venues like the Marty Center's *Sightings* and *Beliefnet.com,* as well as small in-house publications like *Chimes* (the student newspaper at Calvin College) and *Uncompressed,* a 'zine produced by the creative folks in our Student Activities Office. This diverse array of publications has given me the opportunity to speak to a variety of "publics" and I am grateful for the opportunity.

Thanks, also, to John Scherer and Ryan Weberling for their help with the index, as well as their friendship.

I have dedicated this volume to Richard Mouw, who, for me, exemplifies what it means to be a public intellectual who serves the church, and the evangelical family in particular. A long-time philosopher at Calvin College (in fact, I now reside in the office that once was home to Rich), he blazed the trail for someone like me to be able to do just this sort of work from the platform of the Philosophy Department. His work was crucial in demonstrating the importance of "public" scholarship — writing and research undertaken for the sake of readers outside the narrow confines of the guild, and even outside of the academy altogether. His work exhibited (and continues to exhibit) a unique rigor, charity, and generosity that is requisite for research and thinking that is diaconal, undertaken in service to the church. In short, I can get away with spending my time on these sorts of ventures because a generation earlier Rich made the case for its importance in his person and work. Though he has never been my teacher of record, he has been an important mentor and model for me, always a Barnabas, offering encouragement even when he wished I might say things just a bit differently. I am grateful for his example and his friendship.

Finally, I owe a special debt to Jon Pott of Eerdmans: for his encouragement, for engaging lunchtime chats at restaurants around Grand Rapids, and for his willingness to take a risk on this little collection. I hope this venture continues the long and fruitful relationship between Calvin College and Wm. B. Eerdmans Publishing that has been such an important part of the curious and surprising environment that shapes intellectual life in what some might think the most unlikely of places: Grand Rapids, Michigan.

THE CHURCH, CHRISTIAN SCHOLARS, AND *LITTLE MISS SUNSHINE*

THE PIECES COLLECTED here were "occasional" in the sense that they were "invited" in some way: either by an explicit invitation, by an event, or by a situation that I felt needed addressing. Sometimes the request came from colleagues or editors; sometimes the invitation came from students or churches; in other cases the summons came from events — of celebration or tragedy. I have tried to be responsive to such invitations and occasions as a steward of my gifts and expertise. That is, these pieces reflect my settled conviction that Christian scholars have a responsibility to function as public intellectuals for the church *as* "public."

I see philosophy as a deeply *diaconal* discipline: investigating questions that undergird the other disciplines, the work of philosophy serves other fields by undertaking reflection that bears on methodological issues in those other disciplines. (I don't think philosophy reduces to *just* this diaconal role, but I think it is a significant vocation of philosophy.) Significant subdisciplines of philosophy demonstrate this: philosophy of science, philosophy of art, applied ethics, etc. In this respect, my own academic and scholarly vocation — my "guild" work, one might say — has sought to enable philosophy to serve theology (a subdiscipline I describe as "philosophical theology," for short). My calling has been on the boundary between philosophy and theology, using my philosophical training and expertise to serve theology.

But the essays collected here take this diaconal vocation a step further and represent a slightly different tack that has occupied me of late: not just putting philosophy in the service of (academic) theology, but trying to put philosophy in service to the church — to on-the-ground matters of faith, speaking to those who might never darken the door of the academy. Over the past several years I have steadily become more and more convinced that we need to broaden the audience of "Christian scholarship." In the first phase of my scholarly life, I undertook what is often described as "advanced scholarship" or what Pascal Boyer described as "scholarship of discovery": technical work in the discipline aimed at other scholars and disseminated in peer-reviewed journals and scholarly books. In short, I spent my energies writing for that narrow slice of the guild that constituted a circle of expertise (all six of us!). That is an important and needed aspect of Christian scholarship, and I continue to affirm its value. The academic community is an important "public" for Christian scholarship. However, of late I have come to appreciate more and more that this is only one of the publics we are called to address. But there are at least two others: first, the church and wider Christian community; and second, a more general "public" of citizens and neighbors with whom we work, vote, build libraries, and share traffic jams. This collection brings together a number of pieces aimed at the former: the church as "public." In particular, I have been deeply disturbed by a serious vacuum of thoughtful reflection in evangelicalism, and even the constituency of my own denomination. While there are some resources available for thoughtful Christians at a more "popular" level, they tend to be underutilized. In their place our congregations and parishioners are absorbing the kinds of "popular" material that actually undercuts some key elements of Reformed spirituality and practice.

This came home to me in 2005 when President George W. Bush was invited to be the commencement speaker at my home institution, Calvin College. This created quite a furor as a sizeable portion of the faculty, students, and alumni protested his visit, including a page-long advertisement in the local paper denouncing the President's foreign and domestic policies as inconsistent with Christian principles. While this is notable in itself (for more on this, see chapter 11 below), what I found more intriguing and instructive was the reaction received from a vocal part of the variegated community that makes up the so-called "constituency" of the college (alumni, donors, parents, etc.) who were aghast that so-called "Christian" scholars could even entertain such a critique of the President and would see any sort of tension (let alone contradiction) between the Bush administration's foreign and economic policies and a "biblical" worldview. How was it that there could be such a disconnect between what some of the college's leading scholars and teachers thought and what our constituency (made up of mostly alumni who had been taught by these same scholars and teachers) took to be the shape of a Christian worldview?

While one could cite other factors, I'm convinced that one significant reason for this disconnect and distance has been a slow but steady isolation of the scholars from the broader Christian community — which, in this case, is also tethered to a quite specific denominational tradition. In a strange way, the scholars and the "laity" (so to speak) seemed to inhabit parallel worlds that rarely, if ever, intersected. There are a couple of layers to this phenomenon. First, since the late 1970s and into the 1980s, Christian scholars have recognized the importance of breaking out of our Christian ghettoes and speaking to the academic mainstream. Rather than just being teachers at a Christian liberal arts college, there was a sense of obligation — even mission — that demanded much more energy and resources be devoted to making a mark on ("transforming!") the academy as such. Thus Christian scholars at institutions such as my own sought to move from the fringe to the center of their various guilds within the academy. This was undertaken both with a missional emphasis and with at least an implied desire to win respectability for Christian scholarship. And the campaign, one must conclude, has been remarkably successful, particularly in certain disciplines. But one of the prices to pay for such respectability was to adopt a staple stance of academic elitism: an allergic abhorrence for anything "popular," *especially* popular writing. (One of the worst epithets that a scholar can come up with is to describe a colleague as a "popularizer.")

The second layer is a direct result of the first: because all of their energy was devoted to making an impact on the narrower public of the academy, and because the allergy to "popular" writing had seeped into their guild-influenced immune systems, Christian scholars made fewer appearances in the spaces inhabited by, well, "normal" Christians. More time spent at academic conferences meant less time available to speak to adult education classes; more time devoted to publication in specialized scholarly journals meant less time for (and less interest in) publishing in more popular and denominational magazines. And fears of being reduced to a "popularizer" fueled further distance of Christian scholars from the broader Christian community — including even rather proximate communities such as a college's own (denominational) constituency. The result was the creation of a popular vacuum. And nature, we're told, abhors a vacuum — they inevitably demand to be filled.

In the case that hits closest to home for me, as scholars at the denomination's college devoted their intellectual energy to their various guilds, Christians within the denomination found themselves looking for wisdom and guidance where they could get it. The result is that they picked up what was available — in Christian bookstores, magazines, and, perhaps most significantly, on Christian radio. And since Christian intellectuals had pretty much vacated these spaces, the result is that the Christian public began to nourish themselves with what I have to say is a largely unhealthy diet. The irony, for instance, was that the everyday Reformed community that built and sustained Calvin College was actually more influenced by an Arminian Nazarene like James Dobson than they were by the Reformed vision of our best intellectuals. Celebrity pastors, radio evangelists, and Christian talk radio hosts filled the vacuum that was left by the evacuation of Christian intellectuals from the popular spaces of the Christian community. This, I'm convinced, explains the deep disconnect that came to the surface with the President's visit. And the irony, of course, is that most of these constituents had once been our students. Either we were ineffectual teachers (possibly), or we underestimated the fact that a Christian education continues after graduation — and if "we" (Christian scholars) won't provide this life-long learning, then the hunger for guidance and wisdom and insight will be satisfied from other sources. Who are "we" to complain, then, about the popular diet of evangelicalism?

The essays collected in this little book are an archive of my attempts to speak into this vacuum and offer philosophical reflection in the service of faithful discipleship. The impetus to undertake this kind of work stems from what Richard Mouw describes as a "hermeneutic of charity" (in his wonderful little book, *Consulting the Faithful,* which should be required reading for all Christian scholars): a stance that approaches "popular" religion not with suspicion, or condescending cynicism, but with a fundamental affirmation — yea, *love* — for the community of "ordinary" Christians. (Such language of "ordinary" is, of course, rather obnoxious — just the sort of thing that "ordinary" Christians expect from snobby, elitist scholars. As Mouw reminds us, following Kuyper's lead, perhaps the first lesson Christian scholars need to learn is to simply be reminded that they, too, are always already one of *de kleine luyden,* one of the "little people.") One of the worst by-products of the immersion of Christian scholars in the academic mainstream is that we have picked up the condescending habits of the (so-called) secular academy when it comes to our own brothers and sisters. Indeed, the very term "evangelical" can hardly pass our lips without a sneer. For too many Christian scholars, their basic stance toward popular Christianity is derision and condescension. But such a stance will change nothing. I'll be the first to admit that I am often exasperated, frustrated, and embarrassed by my own faith community — that there are days when I can't stomach being described as an "evangelical" because of the guilt by association. But at the end of the day, these are my people. I still pick up *Christianity Today* before I pick up the *Christian Century* or *First Things.* I get the jokes, jabs, and sly references in the orbit of conservative Protestantism. I know and still revere Nonconformist saints like Jim Elliot and Corrie ten Boom. I still understand the inner workings and issues of evangelicalism better than the labyrinthine machinations of American liberalism or Catholicism. I understand why Christians value family, and I sympathize with the struggles of raising children of faith. In short, I still feel at home in evangelical circles — if you understand being "at home" like coming back to a small town Thanksgiving dinner, with all its charm and awkwardness, all its arguments and hugs.

So these are my people, and I'm going to give them the benefit of the doubt. That is what Mouw means by a "hermeneutic of charity," and it's what (I hope) animates this book: the sense that, no matter how much I might disagree and be frustrated by their positions and interpretations, I know that above all my brothers and sisters want to be faithful disciples of Jesus. Even if I think they've bought into all sorts of questionable assumptions and causes; even if I think they've been co-opted by cynical political machines; even though I might think they've assimilated the worst sorts of cultural prejudices; even if I think God wants to invite them to "higher" cultural passions — there is a sense in which I think they're just trying to make their way in the world the best they can. And if they've bought the paradigms sold to them by voices on Christian radio that I think are problematic, then the burden is on *me* to show them otherwise. My responsibility is not to condescendingly look down upon them from my cushy ivory tower, but to take time to get out of the tower and speak to them — and, please note, *learn from them.* Christian scholars would do well to be slow to speak and quick to listen.

This hermeneutic of charity is not just romantic or utopian; in my experience, the wisdom of this stance has been confirmed. When I take the time to teach an adult Sunday school class, I find Christians who are hungry for wisdom. And though ultimately I might be trying to induce a paradigm shift in their thinking, hoping to basically de-program the way Christian radio has got them thinking about gender or justice, I find that so long as I begin from the assumption that folks are interested in knowing what's true, not just what's comfortable, I can invite them to see the world differently. So long as we all begin from the assumption that we want to bring all of our thinking and doing under the Lordship of Christ and the light of the biblical narrative, my brothers and sisters are quite happy to hear a different take on their settled convictions — as long as it is offered in charity and humility, not with scolding and condescension.

This conviction is what motivates me to undertake the work of what we sometimes call a "public intellectual." I think it is crucial that Christian scholars in particular take up this vocation and speak to the church *as* "public." (I think we should also speak to broader constituencies, too; that we should be writing not just for *Christianity Today* and *First Things,* but also for *Harper's* and *Atlantic Monthly.* But that will require jumping a few more hurdles.) This will require us to revalue research and writing that is directed beyond the academy and outside of the guild. It will also require us to spend more time with our (dysfunctional) faith families, and to own up to the fact that we're one of "them" — that, in fact, there's no "us" and "them," there's just "us."

This calling and mission of the Christian public intellectual is pictured, I think, in Jonathan Dayton's and Valerie Faris's surprise hit, *Little Miss Sunshine*. The film invites us to read it allegorically, keying in on Frank, a Proust scholar of international repute who — in order to safely recover from a failed suicide attempt — finds himself stuck in the home of his sister's eclectic family, the Hoovers: father Richard, the down-and-out motivational speaker who is trying (unsuccessfully!) to market his motivational success program; his wife, Sheryl, whose patience for this lark is wearing thin; son Dwayne who has taken a vow of silence and immerses himself in Nietzsche; daughter Olive who, despite her girlish plumpness and awkwardness, is destined for a beauty pageant in California; and Grandpa, Richard's foul-mouthed father who has been ejected from his Arizona retirement community for his lecherous habits (not to mention the heroin use). Into this mix, set in the environment of a tacky bungalow with a staple of fried chicken for dinner, comes Frank, the scholar of French literature. As Dwayne scribbles on his notepad, "Welcome to Hell."

Frank's disdain is barely masked at best. His disgust for his brother-in-law is etched on his face and reveals itself in venomous sarcasm as Frank, who's no doubt published with Cambridge and Yale University Press, is subjected to Richard's description of a publishing deal for his self-help program being worked out in the back room of a conference center in Scottsdale, Arizona. From the moment he enters the house every word of his body language whines, "I can't believe I'm stuck here." This is crystallized in an opening dinner scene that displays the Hoover family in all its glory and ugliness, all its zaniness and dysfunction, all its brokenness and blessing. Paper plates are tossed around the table as Dwayne cracks open the fried chicken, only to have Grandpa enter in a blue-streak of cussing at yet another supper from a box. This is a long way from the university faculty club, and Frank finds himself casting furtive glances at Nietzsche-reading Dwayne as if he were a sort of compatriot, his eyes pleading, "Are you kidding me?" He has entered foreign territory, an alien world — and he's confident he doesn't belong. "Is it always like this?" he asks Dwayne at the close of the evening. "How can you stand it?"

I can't help but see this as an allegory of the Christian scholar, plunked in the middle of church, this gloriously dysfunctional family that constitutes the broken-yet-blessed body of Christ — a people, we might remember, that is not composed of many scholars, opinion-shapers, or those from the upper-crust of elite culture (1 Cor. 1:26). And unfortunately, finding ourselves in the midst of this sort of family, all too often we are given to the haughty disdain exhibited by Frank. We make our way through popular religion as if it were just a bit too icky to touch, as if we really can't believe we're stuck here — and as if we're "better" than that.

Frank's situation intensifies: the family has to make a road trip to Redondo Beach, and since Frank can't be left alone in light of his recent suicide attempt, he too is going to have to cram into the VW van for the interstate adventure across the harsh light of the desert (lighting and backdrop are a very important part of the cinematography in the film). When he's not clawing his way to get out of the VW captivity, he falls into the role of amateur anthropologist, both fascinated and puzzled by this weird people group. When Grandpa goes on a tirade about the importance of sexual exploits to his 15-year-old grandson, Frank's face is contorted by a glare and a stare that communicate both horror and sick fascination, like an onlooker at a car accident. He might be in the van, he might even be biologically connected to this motley crew, but he's not one of them.

But then something changes: when the clutch is shot in the VW bus, the only option is to bump start it by rolling down an incline. Minus an incline, the only hope is to push. And so we see this unlikely team transformed into a human engine, pushing as hard as they can with the side door open so that, as the van fires, the pushers can revert to being passengers by hopping in the open door. The absurdity of this is not lost on Frank who, while they're straining in the dust at the back of the van, announces: "I just want everyone here to know that I am the preeminent Proust scholar in the United States." The implication being, of course: "And I can't believe that I'm stuck here, in the middle of this god-forsaken desert, with these people, pushing a broken-down van, all in order to reach a kitschy, disgusting children's beauty pageant in Redondo Beach, California. *Do you know who I am? Do you have any idea who I am?*"

And yet . . . Frank, too, is taken up in this particular micro-drama of getting the van back on the road. He is alongside the rest of the Hoovers, bent on getting this thing started while also managing to get into it while still moving. This becomes a shared goal, a common good, a *telos* to which they are all now committed with some urgency. And as one by one they make their way back into the rolling van, smiles and laughter break out at the sense of accomplishment. Even Frank falls into a campy drill-sergeant impression: "No one gets left behind!" he shouts in a deep, gravelly voice. "Outstanding, soldier!" he compliments Dwayne, "Out-*standing!*" In what seems surprising to him as well, a beaming smile breaks across his face as he pats the others on the back for a job well done. Granted, his sarcasm and disdain will return when Richard begins rambling about his nine-step program for success, but here we have a first instance of Frank the scholar identifying with the Hoovers, with this zany family that are, at the end of the day, his people. And who, more importantly, he *needs.*

Christian scholars need to push more VW buses with their brothers and sisters. In a very concrete way, we need to find more opportunities to work alongside the faithful who don't attend academic conferences or find solace in the *New York Review of Books.* We need to be reminded that, at the end of the day, we share a common cause and a common confession with all sorts of folk who would embarrass us if we took them along to the MLA convention or the next meeting of the American Historical Society. Being part of the body of Christ represents a task and a mission that divides the world up in curious ways, so that while I might feel much more comfortable with folks who read the *Atlantic Monthly* and can chat with me about the delights of the Parisian literary world, as a member of this strange family that is the church there is a kind of blood-connection that should trump these other identities, scandalous as that may seem. Just as Grandpa Hoover's gruff exterior (almost) conceals his compassionate love for his son and granddaughter, so we should work from a hermeneutic of charity that looks through and past what Rich Mouw describes as "evangelical bad taste." As he puts it in *Consulting the Faithful,* we need "a theology of the 'natural' that is able to recognize dignity in kitsch" — nothing less than a "tacky theology." And we need to reconsider our allegiances and identities. What makes *Little Miss Sunshine* a "family" film that Disney could never dream of is the fact that in it, family ties trump other allegiances. And in fact it is the Hoovers who first exhibit this charity and hostility, welcoming Frank — broken and snobby, elitist and depressed — into their home.

And so we begin to see a transformation in Frank over the course of the film. While he's still not exactly comfortable with this community, he increasingly identifies with them and sees himself as part of the team. When absurdity is piled upon absurdity and he finds himself an accomplice in stealing Grandpa's body from the hospital, he repeats his earlier announcement, but this time as a gesture of poking fun at himself, too: "Did I mention," he asks, "that I'm the preeminent Proust scholar in the United States?" This time, everybody's in on the joke. When they finally arrive at their destination, Frank runs ahead to take leadership and work out the logistics of Olive's entry in the pageant. And when her routine begins to be ridiculed and mocked, Frank is one of the first to jump on the stage in an expression of solidarity, joining in the performance of "Superfreak." Perhaps most significantly, when he and Dwayne are in conversation on the pier, Frank is actually able to play Alain de Botton, reaching out to help Dwayne precisely by drawing on his work as a Proust scholar in a way that is helpful, accessible, and instructive — without being snobby or condescending. In sum, once Frank is reminded of his identification with "these people" — indeed, once he comes to *love* them in all their absurd brokenness, and recognizes that they have loved him in all his own brokenness — he is also in a place to serve them *as* a scholar, to wear his learning more lightly and offer it in a way that is inviting, helpful, constructive, and maybe even loving.

Perhaps the work of a Christian public intellectual should always begin with a confession: that we are given to all sorts of sins and temptations, most notably pride, cynicism, and elitism. Too often we are infected by the same snobbish dismissal as Frank; when we find ourselves amongst "normal" Christians we are, in turns, flabbergasted, appalled, embarrassed, and exasperated. At the same time, they are our Hoovers, so to speak: they are our family, and we hope they will welcome us. We need them, and we need to serve them the best we can with the gifts, skills, and talents that we've been given and that we've cultivated. The essays and articles collected here are some of my attempts to speak and write to audiences outside of the narrow world of the academy, in a mode of servant scholarship or outreach scholarship, convinced that time spent speaking to the church as "public" is just as important as (or even more important than) energy devoted to speaking to the guild.

That's not to say that everything is rosy, that this is easy, or even that I've done a particularly good job. I still wish I had the overwhelming charity and generosity that Rich Mouw exhibits, and in comparison, some of these pieces still feel a bit testy and condescending. I also find some of them still a bit more "highbrow" than most folks at church are going to be comfortable with, and thus the "public" I'm writing for is perhaps still circumscribed quite a bit (though I'll also be quite unapologetic about hoping to invite folks to inhabit the world in ways that rise above the easy amusements encouraged by consumer culture). But I have resisted the temptation to smooth over the warts and revise my voice in collecting them here. I have also resisted the temptation to make them sound smarter or more polished, or to "correct" those places where my mind has changed. Because occasional essays are, by definition, responding to events, situations, and (often last-minute) invitations, such "thoughts out loud" are often penned in haste. I have not tried to remove the inscription of these particular occasions from the pieces as republished here, nor have I tried to eliminate the lingering signs of such compositional haste. Such compositional haste, I think, is an indicator of a kind of writing and scholarship that is trying just to hang on — constrained by an urgency of both time and importance. (The sense of urgency also stems, no doubt, from a twisted kind of vocation: how many Christian scholars and public intellectuals are Jonahs, on the run to Tarshish from what were pastoral callings to Nineveh? Having cut my "public" teeth as a teen-aged itinerant preacher in the Plymouth Brethren, I don't think I've ever quite lost that sermonic accent, preacherly voice, and sense of evangelistic urgency.)

Finally, taking up the work of a Christian public intellectual is not without its costs and risks. I have found the task of thinking in public is a bit risky: the risk of over-simplification; of a 1001 criticisms from scholars for not spending time on the details; of upsetting audiences, administrators, and my wife a time or two; of having to clean up the mess after going public on issue X or Y; of being labeled a "popularizer"; etc. But it would be bourgeois whining to really complain about such things. Instead, I remain grateful for the task and opportunity of trying to be a diaconal scholar, along for the ride in a van with this crazy family that is the body of Christ.

Faith on the Ground: On Discipleship

Chapter 1

WORKING AT REST

So then, a sabbath rest still remains for the people of God; for those who enter God's rest also cease from their labors as God did from his. Let us therefore make every effort to enter that rest, so that no one may fall through such disobedience as theirs. Indeed, the word of God is living and active, sharper than any two-edged sword, piercing until it divides soul from spirit, joints from marrow; it is able to judge the thoughts and intentions of the heart. And before him no creature is hidden, but all are naked and laid bare to the eyes of the one to whom we must render an account.

Hebrews 4:9-13

There is one thing for which I am regularly (and justly) scolded by my wife: I just don't know how to rest. Far too often, we find ourselves talking about my inability to just sit on the couch — without a book, without the TV on, without a notepad in hand, without an agenda of some sort. Rest is something I do very poorly.

Now, in a driven, accelerated culture of achievement and consumption, that might seem like a virtue. One might even be praised for having a "good work ethic" — maybe even a "Protestant" work ethic. So the fact

"Working at Rest," *Perspectives: A Journal of Reformed Thought* 20.5 (May 2005): 8-11. Reprinted with permission.

that I can't seem to rest means that I do get a lot done. Even in the halls of Christian higher education, we place a lot of value on productivity, output, and energy. Admission to college places a value on a busy extracurricular life; college life itself is a whir of activities; and faculty are driven to "produce" good scholarship. But this passage from Hebrews kind of haunts me in that respect. *What if we are created not for output, but rest?*

On the flip side, I find myself often scolding my oldest son who seems to be quite gifted in this respect! Grayson is very happy to just sit on the couch with his mom, or just meander around the house, chit-chatting with whoever might be around. I often bark at him, "Don't you have something to do?! Get a book and read! Do something!" Not only am I terrible at rest, I won't let anyone else rest either.

At the heart of this passage from Hebrews is something that deeply challenges the frenzied busy-ness of our culture — even our so-called "Christian" culture. The writer to the Hebrews has just exhorted these persecuted Christians to not abandon their discipleship. Pointing them to Jesus who is both Apostle and Priest (3:1), he paints a picture of Jesus as a new Moses, a leader who will bring them to a land of promise — which will also be a region of rest. But there is an urgency here, even a "fear" (4:1 KJV) that some will not enter that rest.

The writer addresses this fear by situating it within a story: just as the Israelites were seeking rest in the Promised Land (and many were denied), so we as the people of God are looking forward to a rest. The chronology of the story here is important: the writer invokes the story of Israel, looking forward to rest from their wandering when they arrive in the Promised Land. But then the writer invokes Psalm 95, written long after this settlement in Canaan. So arriving in the Promised Land was only a proleptic foretaste of the rest promised the people of God. Psalm 95, then, still looks forward to another "Sabbath" (v. 9). And "today," the author claims, is the day to enter that rest. But this is where the fear kicks in: like many of the ancient Hebrews, some of these Christians were in danger of not entering this rest. And the same danger exists for us.

So it seems to me that this passage poses a couple of questions:

First, just how would we fail *to enter that rest?*

And second, what would it mean for us to enter *this rest? Just what does it mean for us to "enter* God's *rest" (v. 10)?*

First, what would it mean for *us* to fail to enter this rest? The answer is twofold, or perhaps better, two sides of the same coin: on the one hand, it is *disbelief* that would keep us from entering God's rest (4:2-3); on the other hand, it is *disobedience* that would bar entrance to this rest (4:6, and the force of 3:7-19). How can those two things go together? If it's a matter of belief, we tend to think it is *not* a matter of obedience. We tend to oppose faith and works. But the New Testament does not see belief and obedience as opposed to one another. To be a disciple is to be a disciplined believer. Trust (faith) issues in willing subjection to the Lord. In this case, to *obey* is to learn to *trust* God, and more specifically to learn to *receive* the *gift* of God's rest. To *not* enter would be to refuse this gift of rest by retaining our own frenzied confidence in human effort — trusting in our own labors rather than God's grace.

So, then, what would it mean for us to *enter* that rest? Is this a matter of getting some place? Finding the right location? Is it a matter of waiting for the arrival of the kingdom? While there is a sense in which this rest remains future, there is also an important sense in which it is something we can enter "today," as the writer to Hebrews reiterates. So while there is a chronological anticipation of a rest that is to come, there is also a *kairological* sense to this: we are invited into God's rest "Today!"

Now notice how the writer puts this (4:10): we have the opportunity to enter into *God's* rest. This rest is not merely an abstention from our doing; it is also an entrance into God's rest. This is nothing less than an invitation to *participate* in the life of God. In commenting on this, Calvin notes that "the true rest of the faithful, which is to continue forever, will be when they shall rest as God did. And doubtless as the highest happiness of man is to be united to his God, so ought to be his ultimate end to which he ought to refer all his thoughts and actions." We see, then, that entering God's rest is a matter of how we order our lives: entering God's rest, we might say, is a matter of how we order our desires. Thus Calvin continues by suggesting that to enter God's rest is a matter of *union* with God, and that such union requires a "conformation" and self-denial:

> For here we must always begin, when we speak of a godly and holy life, that man being in a manner dead to himself, should allow God to live in him, that he should abstain from his own works, so as to give place to God to work. We must indeed confess, that then only is our life rightly formed when it becomes subject to God. But through inbred corruption this is never the case, until we rest from our own works; nay, such is the opposition between God's government and our corrupt affections, that he cannot work in us until we rest.

Rest, we might say, is a matter of allowing our "affections" or desires to be disciplined by God. But this is what helps us make sense of what seems to be an abrupt transition in 4:12. Though the writer has focused on "rest," all of a sudden in v. 12 the focus shifts to a powerful metaphor of God's Word as a kind of sword that dissects us. How can we put these two themes together? The point, I think, is this: The exhortation to enter God's rest is bookended by considerations of the Word of God (vv. 1-2; 12-13). And recall that the epistle opens by talking about God's last Word, the Son as the speech of God, or even Jesus as "God's Psalm." The matter of rest is really a matter of *desire,* and the Word is that which both promises and disciplines our desires. Here the Word is pictured as a kind of scalpel that is able to penetrate into our very desires — the "thoughts and intentions of the heart" (4:12). The living power of the Word is able to transform our desires by reshaping our imagination to be directed toward the Triune God. To so desire is to find rest. So entering God's rest is not a matter of doing nothing; it is a matter of desiring the right things, and then ordering our activities in light of that desire. When our desire is ordered to and by the love and grace of God, our autonomous desires to make our mark by our own achievements begin to look empty, even silly.

You'll have to forgive me, but I can't help seeing a whole Augustinian drama played out in this passage. (Admittedly, I see Augustinian themes everywhere. Remind me to tell you about my reading of Pinocchio sometime.) You will remember that for Augustine "rest" was one of the most powerful pictures of our calling as human beings: "You have made us for yourself, and our hearts are restless until they rest in you," he opens the *Confessions* (1.1.1). And he concludes the *Confessions* by inviting us to see that to participate in the life of God is to find repose, exhorting us to find rest in the One who is our rest (13.38.53). And between the opening and closing of the *Confessions* Augustine gives us a glimpse of the exhaustion and restlessness of a life which looks for its final end in anything but the Creator. Augustine documents the almost frenzied pace of his frustrated attempts to find this elusive rest outside of the Triune God.

But I am grateful that in Book 10 of the *Confessions,* after his conversion, Augustine provides a reminder of how even the life of the Christian can remain captive to the exhausting labor of achievement and self-sufficiency. Brothers and sisters, we spurn the gift of God's rest in all kinds of "holy" ways. Indeed, often in the very name of Christ we baptize behaviors that are relentless, exhausting, and ultimately self-asserting, being consumed with "the Lord's work" in a way that rejects his rest. We unwittingly fall back into the anxious frenzy of self-sufficiency, seeking to somehow earn our sanctification. We become exhausted by working so hard at being a worship intern or a residence assistant, or become consumed with making our mark as a Christian scholar, and thus drain our energies in a flurry of projects. In my darker, more Pascalian moments, I wonder if I immerse myself in a 101 "Christian" projects precisely in order to forget that I don't desire God all that much. Sometimes all of our work and busy-ness undertaken with the passion of a "vocation" are just a cover for the fact that we prefer the comfort of ministry pursuits *instead* of the disruptive encounter with the Triune God. Our mundane busy-ness can be a symptom of a spiritual restlessness — a symptom of our own disbelief and disobedience which would prevent us from entering God's rest. When we become consumed with "our work" — whatever that might be, and even if it is noble, holy, and just — we unwittingly fall back into the autonomous dreams of our own making. When we spurn rest, we spurn grace and reject God's gift.

When I used to work in construction, one of the bricklayers gave me a bit of advice: "Work smart, not hard." To enter God's rest does not mean that we'll stop doing things, or that we'll stop working. But I think it does mean that we'll work differently; we'll work smarter. And we'll also learn to rest, because we will have learned that authentic joy is not the product of our autonomous efforts or the outcome of piled up accomplishments; it is the gift of a gracious God who is our rest. This is why I think the ultimate rest — finding our desire in union with God — translates into all kinds of little practices of Sabbath — ways in which we extract ourselves from the world's Herculean attempts at self-fulfillment. That rest which is union with God finds little analogues in my ability to sit quietly in a garden.

Many of us need to work at rest. Of course, that sounds kind of ridiculous, doesn't it? Working at rest? But isn't it interesting that it is just this paradox that the writer to the Hebrews recognizes (4:11)? King James's translation team didn't shrink from the paradox, translating the verse "Let us labour therefore to enter that rest" (KJV). Entering God's rest takes work! It is something we have to learn, and it takes discipline. And I know that I fail regularly: I fail to properly order my desires, and so I fail to let go of my own labors as a supposed source of joy.

The irony of my failure is that this year, I am on sabbatical — a time of Sabbath rest. Judging from my inbox, my Palm Pilot, or my desk, you wouldn't know that. (I really suck at resting.) But this past fall our family spent the semester in Cambridge, England. And I must confess that I have begun to acquire a taste for rest — and I love it! We carved out a way of life that rested from our labors in many ways: we rested from an automobile culture, which meant that we rested both from an oil-driven economics and a frenzied, freeway pace. We enjoyed the rest and leisure of a pedestrian culture, walking and biking everywhere — which takes a little more time, to be sure, but also forces one to inhabit creation in a different way. We rested from the pressures of the PTO and church administration, the labors of American busy-ness and doing all the "right" things for the kids, and rested *in* everyday habits and spaces. I came home for lunch everyday, and Deanna and I enjoyed prawns and baguette for lunch, strolled down to the market, or went to the pub. I took tea breaks every morning and afternoon, and sometimes Dee and I would sip our tea in the garden of Selwyn College and just enjoy the view.

I know that rest is something I have to work at. I'm sure that is true for many of you as well. Be encouraged by the epistle to the Hebrews, which recognizes the paradoxical difficulty of entering *God's* rest: we often need to work at it. Or better, our penchant for self-sufficiency and autonomy means that we will find it hard to receive the *gift* of *God's* rest. We need to work at learning how to receive this gift. I encourage you to find a foretaste of that kingdom rest in mundane ways. Open yourself to the transformative power of the Word; let it transform your desire and imagination; and then enjoy the little daily practices of Sabbath which can be sources of such unspeakable joy.

If we, as the people of God, are called to be a peculiar people, learning to rest will be an important way of distinguishing ourselves from the culture of incessant labor that surrounds us. We will then point our neighbors to the God who is our rest.

Chapter 2
THE SECRET LIVES OF SAINTS:
REFLECTIONS ON DOUBT

But Thomas said to them, "Unless I see the nail marks in his hands and put my finger where the nails were, and put my hand into his side, I will not believe." . . . Then Jesus said to Thomas, "Put your finger here; see my hands. Reach out your hand and put it into my side. Stop doubting and believe."

John 20:25-27

I am a (fairly late) convert to Christian faith. Not raised in the church, my conversion the day after my 18th birthday was a rather "Pauline" experience of a Damascus Road turnaround. As such, my faith has always seemed crystal clear, yea, *certain*. Folks like me find it hard to understand those who wrestle with doubts and questions. In fact, for converts, it becomes very easy to demonize someone like Thomas, to villainize him as a kind of minor Judas. We stand in confident certainty and pronounce: "That'll never be me!"

But my confidence and certainty have been rattled by a couple of things: first, growing in the faith, and going through dark valleys of doubt; and second, raising "second generation" Christians and seeing my children voice questions and doubts that I never felt the permission to voice.

"The Secret Lives of Saints: Reflections on Doubt," *The Banner* (March 2008): 32-33. Reprinted with permission.

So I have come to a new appreciation of Thomas — this doubter who achieved sainthood. The passage that narrates his story (John 20:24-31) is included in the canon of Scripture, I think, in order to give us an encouraging glimpse into the secret lives of saints. I want to offer a meditation on this passage in order to see into the inner life of a saint and to note how Jesus responds to this "doubter." I'd like us to note just three themes or movements in the text.

"Saturday Seasons" in the Christian Life

In 20:24, we note that Thomas wasn't there with the disciples when Jesus first appeared — why might that be?

Recall that the disciples are emerging from that dark "Saturday" — they have seen Jesus die on the cross, seen his body brought down and buried, and must have spent that Saturday thinking the world had ended. The three hours of darkness on crucifixion Friday must have paled in comparison to the dark hopelessness of that Saturday. And it seems that for Thomas — like so many of us — that darkness drove him into hiding and loneliness, away from the friendships he'd forged over the past several years. While the other disciples are huddled together, afraid, commiserating (v. 19), Thomas is elsewhere — no less afraid and miserable, but also alone, and thus easily sucked into the vortex of despair. Imagine Thomas's state of mind when the other disciples come bounding up to him and loudly announce, "We've seen him!" While the darkness of their Saturday has been broken by the inbreaking of resurrection Sunday, Thomas hasn't experienced that yet. And would they really be such joyous believers if they hadn't seen it firsthand? Thomas is still inhabiting the darkness of that despairing Saturday, and the merely "cognitive" announcement that Jesus is risen isn't enough to conquer that darkness.

> A soundtrack for doubt:
> Nickel Creek, "Doubting Thomas," *Why Should the Fire Die?*
> Sara Groves, "Maybe There's a Loving God," *All Right Here*
> Pierce Pettis, "God Believes in You," *Everything Matters*

And so I think it's completely fair — and I think every other disciple would have had the same response — for Thomas to say, "I won't believe it until I put my fingers in the wounds." *Notice,* it won't be enough just to *see* Jesus. What Thomas is struggling with is not just absence, but the *tragedy* of that absence. Jesus didn't die in his sleep — his life was violently taken. And so this one who talked to Thomas about the love of the Father was violently taken from them, abused and tortured, and made to suffer a most horrible death. Who could believe in God after that?

So Thomas announces: "You better not be telling me that Jesus is showing up, perfect and pristine, *as if nothing ever happened!* I won't believe the resurrection unless it's going to be honest about the tragedy I've just witnessed."

I have come to learn that the life of a saint is riddled with dark Saturdays — that we will sometimes endure "Saturday seasons" where our consciousness of the tragic overwhelms and envelops our sense of grace and the goodness of God. But this isn't some sort of "epistemic" doubt of defiance, or a matter of not believing the "evidence." This isn't doubt that stems from not getting our propositions straight. This isn't the "I won't believe it" of defiance but rather the "I *can't* believe it" of despair and hopelessness.

So what happens?

JESUS MEETS US WHERE WE ARE

Notice carefully how the narrative moves forward in verse 26: "a week later. . . ." A week later!! Kierkegaard says that when we read the story of Abraham taking Isaac up Mount Moriah, we fast forward across one little remark: that it took *three days.* Having been shaped by ESPN highlight reels, we sometimes underestimate the slow-motion nature of real life, the life inhabited by biblical characters. And so we need to slow down and note that opening of verse 26: a week passes in which Thomas is left in this state. It's as if he is left to a week of dark Saturdays. What must he have experienced during that time? Some of you know.

But what does Jesus do with Thomas's doubt? Jesus shows up; Jesus meets Thomas where he is. Jesus comes to Thomas, speaks peace into his life, and then invites him to wrestle with his doubts — in a way, to wrestle with God the way Jacob did. And so Jesus invites Thomas to touch his scars, to enter into the grotesque and put his hands *into* the wounds. I think there are a couple of important lessons embedded here.

First, I would suggest that Thomas's so-called doubt is a kind of brutally honest faith. Unlike those versions of "faith" that confuse themselves with certainty, Thomas is up-front and honest about the tragic nature of a broken world — the sort of world that would crucify its Creator. Thomas doesn't want an "easy" faith that ignores the tragic; the only faith he's interested in is one that goes *through* the tragic, the grotesque, the wounds of the world. This, I'm convinced, is a central feature of the secret lives of saints. Saints experience the depth and richness of God's grace precisely because their faith hangs precariously at that point where the tragic is always present. Our broken world is poised on a precarious fulcrum and wobbles between glory and the grotesque, beauty and brokenness, grace and tragedy. Saints are those who live their faith close to this tottering hinge — because it's only by being close enough to see the world's pain that we can ever hope to see God's face in the same world. Those who confuse faith with certainty stay as far away from the fulcrum as they can.

Second, notice God's response: God *absorbs* such doubts and questions. God meets us where we are, with all of our doubts. And he doesn't paper over the tragedy of our Fridays and Saturdays. The tragic and broken is *taken up* in the inbreaking of resurrection Sunday — and the inbreaking of resurrection faith. It isn't ignored; it's not "as if it never happened." Rather, the risen Jesus meets Thomas where he is and invites him to *touch the tragic,* to put his hands in the wounds. Jesus doesn't pretend it was otherwise. God is not afraid of our doubts, and he isn't interested in giving us a faith that acts as if there's no tragedy.

BLESSED IS *BELIEVING*, NOT CERTAINTY

Jesus exhorts Thomas no longer to be unbelieving, but to be believing (the tense is of interest here). And then he remarks: "Blessed are those who have not seen and yet have believed." Jesus is speaking to us, and this is intended not to villainize Thomas, but to encourage us. Jesus encourages us by suggesting that believing is *blessed;* but it is important for us to keep in mind that believing is not certainty. Our absorption in modernity has gotten us confused on this point.

Kierkegaard, perhaps the patron saint of doubting believers, once said that "Doubt comes into the world through faith." Doubt is not the antithesis or antidote to faith; it is its companion in a way. We might simply put it this way: *Only believers can doubt.* And in some cases, doubt is faithful precisely where certainty is *un*faithful. Some of our doubts — like Thomas's — grow out of our believing the promises of a good and loving God. The lament psalms (e.g., Psalm 77) articulate just this kind of strange paradox: that it is sometimes more faithful to doubt precisely when it seems like God's goodness has been eclipsed by the tragic. It's not that we won't believe, but we *can't* believe.

And at those moments, I think God shows up, like Jesus to the disciples, and in a quiet way says "Yes!" to our doubts and questions and cognitive dissonance. God meets us where we are, and in doing so affirms that sometimes even doubt is faithful. That is one of the secrets in the lives of saints like Thomas.

Chapter 3
ARE MEN REALLY WILD AT HEART?

with Mark Mulder

HAVE RIFLE SALES started to soar at the local Wal-Mart? Are friends discussing white water rafting and rock climbing for the first time? Are council meeting disagreements now settled with fisticuffs instead of votes? If you answered yes to one or more of the previous questions, chances are that the men in your community have just finished reading John Eldredge's *Wild at Heart: Discovering the Secret of a Man's Soul* (Thomas Nelson, 2001). And your community is not alone: the book has sold over a million copies and spawned a cottage industry of retreats, conferences, and spin-off products. It has also been the focus of men's Bible studies both at churches and on college campuses across America. Our interest in the *Wild-at-Heart* phenomenon was triggered by the attention the book was receiving in dorms on campus, as well as in local churches.

Eldredge has delivered a book that rightly delineates the necessity for husbands to love their wives and for fathers to be intimately involved in raising their children. Beyond that, he correctly searches to discover that certain something that we're all longing for. In addressing the latter quest, he insightfully notes that men live lives feeling unfulfilled, searching to satisfy a vaguely unsettling malaise. The Irish musical group U2 articulated this longing well when they crafted the song, "I Still Haven't Found What I'm Looking For." Unfortunately, while Eldredge has asked

"Are Men Really Wild at Heart?" with Mark Mulder, *Perspectives: A Journal of Reformed Thought* 19.8 (October 2004): 18-22. Reprinted with permission.

the right questions, he ultimately offers sometimes misguided and at other times patently wrong solutions.

In particular, we are concerned that the embrace of *Wild at Heart* by men in the Christian Reformed Church is a symptom of a wider phenomenon: an accommodation to broader cultural forces, including an embrace of generic evangelical theology and practice which, upon closer inspection, is at odds with the distinctives of biblical, Reformed faith and practice. Let's first consider the shape of Eldredge's proposal that men are "wild at heart."

MANHOOD AS AN ADVENTURE

In *Wild at Heart,* Eldredge argues that men have been emasculated — they've been told by the church and society in general that they should be "responsible, sensitive, disciplined, faithful, diligent, dutiful, etc." (xi). These are all fine qualities, according to Eldredge, but they stifle and constrain men from being what they really are: wild and dangerous. The restlessness that he suggests all men feel is due to the confusion engendered when society asks them to act like women while the church asks them to be "Really Nice Guys." Both have conspired to cheat men of the opportunity to be William Wallace (as portrayed by Mel Gibson in the film *Braveheart*), demanding instead that they act like Mother Teresa. Eldredge counsels his readers to search their hearts, confident that they will find three universal desires: a battle to fight, an adventure to live, and a beauty to rescue.

In essence, all men have a battle to fight because they have been "hardwired" for it — it is part of the "masculine design" (10). As evidence of this supposedly natural instinct within men, Eldredge cites the phenomenal commercial success of combat films like *High Noon, Saving Private Ryan,* and *Die Hard* and declares that it was men, not women, who flocked to the theaters and video stores. Eldredge takes the seemingly universal penchant of our sons to construct guns out of sticks, Lego, and napkins as further evidence of this universal ferocity.

Similarly, all men have a need to live the adventurous life. This is why Eldredge's sons attempt to rappel from the second-story window of his house, why the western cowboy has taken on mythic proportions in the US, and why men get much more excited about seeing the latest Steven Segal flick than they do about going to Bible study.

Finally, Eldredge suggests, all men have an inherent desire to rescue a beauty. Echoing the chivalry of medieval romance, Eldredge contends that nothing inspires a man like a beautiful woman: she makes a man want to be a hero. The fact that the woman, in turn, "yearns to be fought for" (p. 16) ensures that the process is full of synergy.

We could engage this book on a number of levels. Here we want to consider just a few.

CREATION AND MANHOOD: IS WAR GOOD?

One of the core themes of the Reformed tradition — and one of its accents that it offers to the larger body of Christ — is a distinct theology of creation. At the heart of the tradition is an affirmation that "the whole world belongs to God." This stems from the fundamental biblical affirmation that creation is *good* (Gen. 1:31). The reason we can affirm the spheres of art and politics, economics and recreation is that these are part of a good creation. This is not only an affirmation about the past — about a long-lost origin; it is also our fundamental hope for the future. All things are being restored to this goodness. Redemption is the foretaste of the creational goodness, and we are called to be agents of such restoration. Like the dove who brought back an olive leaf to the ark — bringing hope — so we as the church are to bring foretastes of the kingdom to a broken world.

But what does it mean to say that creation is "good"? Well, one important aspect of the goodness of creation is *harmony* or peace. God's creation is a place where we certainly find difference — different kinds of creatures, differences between men and women — but these differences are related in harmony. The original *shalom* of creation is characterized by both a lack of conflict and an abundance of flourishing. The Fall introduced enmity and conflict into the peace of a good creation (Gen. 3:15). But this is precisely why redemption is concerned with the restoration of peace and the undoing of conflict. This is pictured most powerfully in the prophecies of Isaiah, who paints a picture of swords being beaten into plowshares (Isa. 2:4) and wolves lying down with lambs (11:6-7). This is not just about the end of the defense industry or a global petting zoo: redemption is the promise of a renewed creation in which every facet of enmity, violence, and war is erased precisely because it was never part of what God intended for creation.

Now, what does this theology of creational harmony have to do with *Wild at Heart*? Well, if we read carefully, we will see that Eldredge offers a theology of creation that is diametrically opposed to the vision we've just sketched. First, we must appreciate that he stakes his account of "manhood" on a notion of how God made us; in other words, he tries to suggest that his account of manhood is rooted in creation. The book is riddled with claims about "how God made" men and women, making claims about the "essence" of little boys and girls.

But what Eldredge attributes to *creation* biblical Christianity ascribes to the *Fall!* Eldredge wants to inscribe war into the very hearts of men: "the warrior," he tells us, "is hardwired into every man" (p. 141). For Eldredge, men are *made for war* — indeed, *created* for war. Men can only be men where there are battles to fight! Battle, war, and enmity are thus inscribed into the very structure of creation.

But if battles are the fruit of enmity and conflict, and such enmity is a result of the Fall, not creation, then it cannot be the case that being a warrior is essential to being a man. (What will men do in the kingdom — when peace reigns and the swords are beaten into plowshares?) Eldredge actually ends up endorsing a consequence of the Fall *as if* it were part of God's good creation. To endorse the warrior-ideal that he does actually fosters sinfulness, not redemption. Eldredge wants to keep all the swords in the shape of weapons, but the prophetic vision of redemption sees them transformed into plowshares.

WILLIAM WALLACE OR JESUS OF NAZARETH: WILL THE REAL MAN PLEASE STAND UP?

While Eldredge wants the hero of his book to be God, it's hard to avoid the conclusion that the real hero is William Wallace of *Braveheart* fame.

(Bruce Willis's *Die Hard* films are a close second. And the incarnation of "The Rock" in *Walking Tall* would be a favorite.)

But given the picture of manhood that Eldredge has painted as that intended by our Creator, we found ourselves asking: "Is *Jesus* a man?" How can men be warriors at heart when we see the model of Jesus' non-resistance?

Wild at Heart anticipates this problem by holding up God as the very paragon of manhood. Just as he suggested that men are warriors at heart, so he argues that God is a kind of transcendent Braveheart (p. 35), concluding that "there is something fierce in the heart of God" (p. 29). But this theology runs into a couple of significant problems.

First, Eldredge wants us to believe that his picture of manhood is deduced from his theology of God's nature, but actually the logic runs something like this: we are created to be warriors; we are created in the image of God; therefore, God is a warrior. In other words, we worry that Eldredge's picture of God as the paradigmatic warrior, adventurer, and rescuer is, in fact, reading a fiction back *into* God. In addition to painting a deficient picture of God as *needing* adventure (as if God could lack something), most significantly Eldredge's theology makes God essentially a warrior, and by doing so inscribes conflict into the very heart of God. (Eldredge's account is very un-Trinitarian.) In other words, Eldredge fails to distinguish between God's relation to a *fallen* world and God's very essence.

Second, Eldredge's theology has a big problem: *women*. He wants us to deduce that men are essentially warriors because God is a warrior and we are created in God's image. But wait a minute: *women* are created in God's image, too (Gen. 1:27). So shouldn't that mean that women are "made" to be warriors, too? Well, no, Eldredge replies: "the masculine and feminine run throughout all creation" (p. 35). And, in fact, God also has all of the "feminine" traits as well (he wants to be loved, wants an adventure to share, and has a beauty to unveil). But if that's the case, what exactly are the clues as to which of these divine traits men are to emulate and which women are to model?

Is it not rather the case that men and women are called *together* and in the same way to be disciples of Jesus, bearers of the divine image? And do we not find the traits of the divine image encapsulated in the fruit of the Spirit — love, joy, peace, patience, kindness, goodness, faithfulness, gentleness, and self-control (Gal. 5:22-23)? Do we see such fruit from William Wallace? Do we not see these most powerfully embodied in Jesus of Nazareth?

A UNIVERSAL LONGING

As we've suggested, Eldredge assumes that this quest is a uniquely male pursuit. (Women never get to have their own adventure; they only get to *share* an adventure.) He asks the reader to allow him to "bypass the entire nature vs. nurture 'is gender really built-in?' debate" (p. 8). With a tenuous interpretation of Genesis 1:27, he charges ahead with the assumption that men's and women's *biological* distinctions inherently make them radically different *social* beings. If he is correct about the so-called "hardwired" nature of men, why then do some societies expect drastically different behaviors of men than others? How is it possible that some societies associate what Western cultures would assume to be feminine characteristics with men? So the "nature vs. nurture" question cannot be avoided so easily. As we've already noted, from a biblical perspective, despite biological differences, all humans — women and men — are called to image God by bearing the fruit of the Spirit. And the Bible encourages us to see that such is the product of formation or nurture: disciples aren't born, they're made.

Eldredge, however, insists that there is a spiritual restlessness that's somehow unique to men (p. 5). Such an assertion assumes that men and women have distinctly different methods of fulfillment. Is it not rather that all *humans* have an emptiness that can be best described as what U2 names a "God-shaped hole"?

Moreover, Eldredge's method here once again confuses creation and Fall. He urges men to look into their hearts and find "written" there three desires: for a battle to fight, an adventure to live, and a beauty to rescue (p. 9). And in view of the new covenant promise (Jer. 31:33), he urges us to trust our hearts. But while it is true that we are a "new creation" (2 Cor.

5:17) and have been renewed by the Spirit (Rom. 8:4), it does not follow that desires for battle and adventure are the fruit of this new heart. In fact, in these contexts Paul says exactly the opposite: being a new creation makes us ambassadors of *reconciliation* not enmity (2 Cor. 5:17-20), and the heart set on the Spirit seeks *peace* not conflict (Rom. 8:6).

COUNTERCULTURAL, OR HOLLYWOOD BAPTIZED?

Finally, although Eldredge presents his work as countercultural, it ultimately falls short of seriously undermining the status quo. In fact, *Wild at Heart* could probably be described as simple accommodation at best and pandering at worst. (In our more cynical moments, we fear *Wild at Heart* is just religious gobbledy-gook to give men "spiritual" reasons to go hunting and fishing every weekend!)

Eldredge offers little to subvert the archetype of the macho man personified *ad nauseam* in popular movies by Bruce Willis and Sylvester Stallone, among a whole host of others. It remains difficult to discern what's so revolutionary about what Eldredge is offering. While he writes as if he is upsetting cultural norms, he's actually perpetuating the notion of the "manly man" that's been in place for centuries, giving us a kind of *Iron John* for Christians. Routinely the protagonists of these films are men who have been deeply wounded and are initially unwilling to respond when called into their "battle to fight." They universally respond with a vengeance and along the way manage to somehow meet Eldredge's requirement "to rescue beauty" (usually a voluptuous damsel incapable of mustering her own defense, much less intelligent conversation). It could be compellingly argued that *Wild at Heart* has simply taken the rote script of nondescript action movies, justified it with questionable scriptural hermeneutic, and presented it as God's plan for Christian men.

Beyond that, and as already alluded to, Eldredge does note that women have a role to play in this drama: they are there to be rescued by strong men — it's universal to human nature, he claims (p. 181). What do women need to be rescued from? Basically, insecurity: Eldredge writes that "every woman needs to know that she is exquisite and exotic and chosen" (p. 182). How can she elicit that kind of rescue from a man? The answer: "She seduces him. She uses all she has as a woman to arouse him to be a man" (p. 191). The ultimate example of proper seduction, he suggests, was Ruth and Boaz. God sets that template for all women to follow when "he not only gives Ruth her own book in the Bible but also names her in the genealogy" (p. 191).

Again, questionable biblical interpretation aside, such notions only perpetuate the cultural status quo. Eldredge's recipe for female fulfillment hardly diverges from that of the makers of the Barbie Doll or the franchisers of Hooter's restaurants. Rather than offering a subversive and invigorating message for a woman, Eldredge has endorsed the exploitative and oppressive conception that objectifies her sexuality and communicates that she has value only in her relationship to a man — insinuating that men and women cannot be completely whole unless engaged in some sort of romantic relationship. Such a notion seems contradictory to 1 Corinthians 7 where Paul extols the virtues of singleness, noting that in singleness the Christian becomes more dependent on life within the larger family of God. This is not to deny, of course, that marriage is a kind of sacrament — a means of grace by which many are sanctified. But even then, the relation is not one of dependence as suggested by Eldredge.

A COUNTERCULTURAL GOSPEL

With all this said, Eldredge should be applauded for asking questions about the lack of fulfillment American Christians experience in the twenty-first century. Unfortunately, however, we feel that men and women who follow his prescription will still not find what they're looking for. In *Wild at Heart,* Eldredge has convoluted Scripture to the point that war instead of peace is seen as the ideal state of human relations, and Jesus is the brigadier general of a host of 10,000 armed and trained angels instead of the teacher who proffered the revolutionary ideas of meekness, mercifulness, and peacemaking.

Moreover, Eldredge's argument, though couched as countercultural, actually sustains a flawed caricature that ultimately inhibits men from fully realizing who they are in Christ. Perhaps most perilously, *Wild at*

Heart both implicitly and explicitly minimizes the consequences of sin and the Fall. To argue that there are separate "secrets" for men and women in finding spiritual contentment suggests a kind of "self-help" strategy that ignores the deep reality — and necessity — of grace.

Instead, we ought to hear the gospel's call to men and women as a call to a deeply countercultural identity: while appreciating our differences, together (Gal. 3:28) we are to find our identity in the Crucified One who did not assert his own interests (Phil. 2:1-11). To be a peculiar people of peace and love, a holy nation distinguished by kindness and gentleness — that is the gospel's truly countercultural calling, for both men and women, as disciples of Jesus.

Chapter 4

POPE JOHN PAUL II:
A PROTESTANT'S APPRECIATION

THE PASSING OF Pope John Paul II into eternal life is not only a loss for the Roman Catholic Church; it is a loss for Christians of all traditions and confessions. Indeed, though I trace my confessional identity to the Reformation protest against "Rome," it was John Paul II who reminded me that to be Christian is to be catholic.

Pope John Paul II articulated what papal biographer George Weigel describes as "the catholic difference"; that is, the Pope unapologetically asserted that to confess Jesus is Lord is to see the whole world differently. Thus the Pope's vision of catholicism is what Weigel calls an "optic": "a way of seeing things, a distinct perception of reality" that made a difference. But this was a *catholic* difference: on the one hand, this vision was generous and ecumenical, such that Christians from across traditions and around the globe could join together to proclaim the gospel to the modern world. It is no surprise, then, that Pope John Paul II was committed to reconciliation, overseeing the most comprehensive commitment to religious dialogue in the history of the Vatican — including fruitful dialogue between Rome and the churches of the Reformation. (This passion was articulated in his 1995 encyclical *Ut Unum Sint.*) On the other hand, this catholic vision was *different.* The gospel proclaims that the whole world belongs to God and that this makes a difference: for the way

---

"Pope John Paul II: A Protestant's Appreciation," *Dubuque Telegraph Herald,* April 10, 2005. Reprinted with permission.

we think about justice; economic distribution; our relation to material goods, human relationships, and bodies; and even how we think about suffering. So the Pope was also unabashed in his assertion of this difference, never shy to articulate a prophetic critique of what he saw as the creeping "culture of death" taking hold of the modern world, whether in the oppressive form of Communism which he helped topple, or in the form of America's persistent use of the death penalty and unjust military interventions. The Pope's prophetic vision of the gospel's impact on every sphere of life helped those of us who are Reformed to be reminded that ours is a catholic vision.

The Pope's vision will forever be known as one committed to the "culture of life" as opposed to the culture of death. Unlike the simplistic versions of this bandied about in American party politics, Pope John Paul II left us with a rich philosophical and theological articulation of this moral vision in encyclicals such as *Evangelium Vitae* and *Veritatis Splendor*. At the heart of this was a theology of the body that could affirm all the goods of embodiment, from the arts to sexuality, in a way that avoided the puritanical gnosticism of much of evangelicalism. And in his final years the Pope modeled for us a profound theology of suffering, trying to show a modern world that, despite all our pretensions to mastery and control, there is redemption to be found by living out of control and receiving grace from a God of great gifts.

Christians of all confessions, and perhaps especially Christians from the so-called "Reformed" churches, should take time this week to give thanks to our giving God for the gift of John Paul II. We would do well to learn to see the world through the optic of "the catholic difference."

Chapter 5
TEACHING A CALVINIST TO DANCE: ON BEING REFORMED AND PENTECOSTAL

IT CAN BE a little intimidating to admit that one is Pentecostal in a Reformed context. It's a bit like being at the ballet and letting it slip that you're kind of partial to NASCAR and country music. Both claims tend to a clear a room. And yet, I find myself happily defining myself as a Reformed charismatic, a Pentecostal Calvinist.

It's been said that testimony is the poetry of Pentecostal experience, so permit me to begin with a personal poem that might provide some background. I wasn't raised in the church; rather, I was quite "miraculously saved" the day after my 18th birthday through my girlfriend (now wife!) doing a little missionary dating. I received my earliest formation in the Plymouth Brethren, in a sector that defined itself as *anti*-Pentecostal and took a certain pride in knowing that the "miraculous" gifts had ceased to function with the death of the last apostle. Through a path that is convoluted and riddled with hurts, our spiritual pilgrimage eventually took us across the threshold of a Pentecostal church where we were welcomed, embraced, and transformed.

And there, in that Pentecostal church in Stratford, Ontario — once home to Aimee Semple McPherson — God showed up. As I encountered him in ways I hadn't experienced or imagined before, God shook my intellectual frameworks and rattled my spiritual cage at the same time.

"Teaching a Calvinist to Dance," *Christianity Today* (May 2008): 42-45. Reprinted with permission.

But let me add one more layer to this story: at the same time that I was being immersed in the Spirit's activity and presence in Pentecostal spirituality, and being formed and embraced by charismatic worship, I had started a master's degree in philosophical theology at the Institute for Christian Studies, a graduate school in the Dutch Reformed tradition at the University of Toronto. So my week looked a bit odd: Monday to Friday I was immersed in the intellectual resources of the Reformed tradition, diving into the works of Augustine, Calvin, Kuyper, and Dooyeweerd. Then on Sunday we'd show up at the Pentecostal church where, to be honest, things got pretty crazy sometimes. It was a long way from Toronto to Stratford, if you know what I mean — about the same distance from Geneva to Azusa Street.

For a lot of folks, that must sound like trying to inhabit two different space-time continuums. But in fact, I never experienced much tension between these things. Of course, the church and my academic world didn't bump into one another; the world of my Pentecostal experience didn't run into the world of my Reformed philosophical and theological investigations. Dooyeweerd and Jack Hayford don't often cross paths. But in a way, I felt that they met *in me* — and they seemed to fit. There was some deep resonance I experienced between the two.

In fact, I would suggest that being charismatic actually makes me a better Calvinist; my being Pentecostal is actually a way for me to be more Reformed. Let me unpack this in two themes.

SOVEREIGNTY AND SURPRISE

Reformed folk praise, value, honor, and make central the sovereignty of God. The theological giants of the Reformed tradition — Calvin, Edwards, Kuyper, and others — have put God's sovereignty at the center and heart of a Reformed "world- and life-view." God is the sovereign Lord of the cosmos; God is free from having to meet our expectations; God is sovereign in his election of the people of God. God's sovereignty is one of the pillars of the Reformed "accent" in the Christian tradition.

I think there is an interesting way in which Pentecostals live out a spirituality that takes that sovereignty really, really seriously. In particular, I think Pentecostal spirituality and charismatic worship takes the sovereignty of God so seriously that you might actually be *surprised* by God every once in a while. If you're Pentecostal, you take the sovereignty of God so seriously that you are open and expectant that the Spirit of God is sometimes going to surprise you because God is free to act in ways that might differ from *your* set of expectations that you've been bringing to the encounter.

In fact we can see this right in the DNA of the church and right at the very heart of Pentecost. The church, you'll remember, is "genetically" pentecostal. The birthplace of the church that makes us the body of Christ is Pentecost. You'll also recall that some pretty strange stuff happened at Pentecost, strange enough that others didn't know what to make of it and so concluded that the apostles were drunk! But what I find really interesting about Pentecost and about St. Peter's pentecostal spirituality is not just that he's participating in the surprise of the Spirit, but that he has the courage to stand up and say, "This is what the Spirit was talking about" (Act 2:16). His horizons are overwhelmed enough, and he is open enough to God doing something new and different, that he eventually has the courage to stand up and, in the face of the madness that is Pentecost Sunday, boldly proclaim, "This is God!" When Jesus ascended and promised the Spirit, I don't imagine the disciples expected the scene that unfolded at Pentecost. And yet Peter exhibits an openness to God surprising our expectations.

The heart and soul of that pentecostal spirituality is not the "stuff," the manifestations, but rather the courage and openness and expectancy to see and say that God is *in* those manifestations — that God is in the surprises — and to say, "This is what the Spirit promised."

That means taking seriously God's sovereignty in worship in ways that have to be learned. I think as Reformed folk we are absolutely committed to God's sovereignty. But ironically, our worship doesn't often reflect this. This is because we have learned habits of worship that effectively constrain the sovereignty of God, that have highly defined and narrow expectations of the Spirit's operations. Thus I imagine a kind of "Pentecostalized" Reformed spirituality that loosens up our expectations so that we expect the sovereign Lord to show up in ways that might surprise us. If we take our own Reformed convictions about God's sovereignty seriously, then we can, with Peter, be boldly open to the Spirit's surprise. We need not immediately kick back into fear, but instead be open to seeing God at work in what might sometimes appear to be the madness of Pentecost, and have the courage to say the Spirit is at work there.

I think that's exactly the sort of sensibility that is embodied in Jonathan Edwards, America's greatest theologian. The Puritan preacher, reading monotone from his pulpit (sermons that were labyrinthine theological treatises), would at the same time be witnessing strange manifestations, convulsing bodies, shouts and yelps, surprising works of the Spirit of God. But Edwards the Reformed theologian is discerning enough not to just write this off but to say, "There's something of the Spirit at work in this." So Pentecostal spirituality, we might say, extends the Calvinist conviction about the sovereignty of God to worship in a way that is open to, even expects, the sovereign Lord to surprise us.

THE GOODNESS OF CREATION AND EMBODIED WORSHIP

Reformed folk, particularly in the Dutch tradition of Kuyper and Dooyeweerd, often emphasize the "goodness of creation" — that God created a material universe that he pronounced was "very good" (Gen. 1:31). And although it is fallen, God is redeeming this world, not redeeming us *out* of it. An important piece of that affirmation is the goodness of embodiment — the goodness of materiality, of the stuff we bump into, of the bodies we inhabit.

But that's precisely why I've always found it a bit strange that Reformed worship so often treats human beings as if we're brains-on-a-stick. All week long we talk about how good creation is, how good embodiment is, but then we have habits of worship that treat us as if we're brains-on-a-stick, merely depositing great ideas in our heads in order to make us into rather cerebral disciples. Despite all our talk about the goodness of creation and embodiment, in Reformed worship the body doesn't show up that much.

Pentecostals, on the other hand, *embody* their spirituality. In fact, there's a sense in which Pentecostal worship is the extension of the Reformed intuition about the goodness of creation and the goodness of embodiment. We can see this in just a few examples.

First, Pentecostals believe in healing — and they don't mean merely "spiritual" healing. They mean the physical healing of bodies. They think that's part of what the cross accomplishes. And implicit in that practice is an affirmation that God cares about our bodies. God doesn't want to just save your soul. God also cares about your body. The Pentecostal emphasis on the healing of the body is a working out of that affirmation of the goodness of embodiment.

Second, Pentecostals use their whole bodies in worship. Pentecostal worship can get a little messy; indeed, sometimes there are bodies everywhere! On a more microcosmic scale, I can still remember the first time I ever raised my hands in worship — there in that Pentecostal church in Stratford. Tentatively and awkwardly raising your arms, hands trembling, you feel like an idiot — and, of course, that's precisely the point. To be in a position with hands outstretched, or prostrate on the floor, is to be in a position of vulnerability and humility. And that can be an especially powerful spiritual discipline for Reformed Christians who are probably prone to a certain staid confidence in our intellectual prowess and doctrinal precision. I thank God for those practices of embodied humiliation that are part and parcel of Pentecostal worship; they were exactly the counterweight I needed as a young Reformed philosopher. But they were also an embodiment of the theories I was absorbing. Pentecostals take seriously what Reformed folk talk about when it comes to the goodness of embodiment.

There is a third sense in which Pentecostals embody the Reformed affirmation of embodiment: it's in *touch*. When Pentecostals pray for one another, we *touch* one another. We lay hands on our sister or brother. Pentecostal worship always involves times of dedicated periods of prayer — "altar time" that brings together the people of God with hands clasped, embraced in prayer, laying on hands in hope. There's something being channeled and charged when the community expresses itself in that kind of touch.

So Pentecostals live out both the Reformed emphasis on the sovereignty of God and the Reformed affirmation of the goodness of embodiment. That's why I don't experience much tension between these core aspects of Reformed identity and charismatic spirituality.

The church's DNA is pentecostal. And one of the exciting things about living and inhabiting pentecostal spirituality is that it is an invitation to also worship with the rest of the world. The explosion of the Spirit's work in world Christianity looks like pentecostal spirituality. It is important for Reformed Christians not to be scared of that, and in fact to see in that an invitation of the Spirit to live out the Reformed intuitions we talk about all the time.

Chapter 6
THE ARCHITECTURE OF ALTRUISM:
ON LOVING OUR NEIGHBOR(HOOD)S

WHEN JESUS SUMMARIZES the "greatest commandment," it is a two-fold obligation that hinges on *love:* "You shall love the Lord your God with all your heart" and "You shall love your neighbor as yourself" (Luke 10:27, echoing Lev. 19:18). It is intriguing to me that when Jesus points to the centrality of *love,* he also invokes a metaphor which is not familial (e.g., "brother" or "friend") or ethnic (e.g., "your people"), but almost geographical: we are to love *the neighbor* — the one next to us, who happens (by providence) to be in proximity. The neighbor could be a friend or an enemy, a foreigner or a brother. The call to love the neighbor is a call to love all of them — that is why all of Jesus' injunctions to love are taken up in the call to love the neighbor.

But if we're honest, the geography of this injunction must sound strange for a culture that dwells in "executive" homes on cul-de-sacs with heated garages and massive decks in the backyard. North American culture increasingly inhabits the kind of world where we not only don't know our neighbors — we never even see them. Many denizens of late modern culture emerge bleary-eyed from bed before dawn, grab a travel mug of coffee while running out the door into the attached garage, clicking the automatic opener to begin the daily commute. According to the most recent *Commuting in America* III report, for 75 percent of people this

"The Architecture of Urban Altruism: Loving our Neighbor(hood)s," *Comment* (September 2007): 61-64. Reprinted with permission.

is a journey that happens alone, in a private vehicle. So we begin our day in isolation: the transition from home to garage to vehicle to expressway is insulated from any contact with others. When we get home, there's little difference. The culture of automobility engenders a residential architecture where the three-car garage swallows almost the entire front elevation, leaving a small gap for a front door — but eliminating any room for an expansive front porch. Instead, houses are set back from the street, guarded by the fortress-like wall of garage doors, leaving us to retreat to the privacy of fenced backyards and sprawling decks — once again, insulated by pressure-treated lumber from any contact with our neighbors. Thus our suburban "neighborhoods" are all too often collections of privatized insulated pods that secure us from any contact with "neighbors." In such a world, Jesus' command sounds a tad anachronistic and strange.

So what would it mean to take seriously Jesus' injunction to love our *neighbors?* How could we recover a sense of the proximity of love? And how could we take seriously the geography of this ethical vision? If Jesus' vision of agapic love hinges on love of the neighbor, then shouldn't we think seriously about how this plays itself out in the very real, incarnate, concrete proximity of our neighbor*hoods?* How could we connect Jesus' commandment to love our neighbor with Jeremiah's prophetic vision of "seeking the welfare of the city" (Jer. 29:7)?

In *The Architecture of Happiness,* philosopher Alain de Botton explores the way in which the built environment either fosters or detracts from the pursuit of happiness and fulfillment. Jesus' vision is a call beyond such eudaimonism, but Botton is onto something: because we are embodied, physical, yea "incarnate" creatures, the material conditions of our dwelling shape and mold us more than we often realize. Christian exhortations to love our neighbors usually amount to encouragements to muster the will power to care about others — a call to a resolute interiority and attitude. But what if Christian neighbor-love had a structural, material concern at its base: that we care about the very physical shape of our residential dwelling and critically consider how the material conditions of our built environment foster or detract from love of neighbor? In a world where the built environment threatens to squelch the very category of "neighbor," might not we heed Jesus' command precisely by being concerned to build communities that encourage encounters with neighbors? Could there be an architecture of neighbor-love? While Botton's architecture of happiness strikes me as a bit self-absorbed, might we nonetheless be concerned — as Christians — with an *architecture* of altruism?

While Botton's recent book is an interesting prompt in this regard, my thinking along these lines has been significantly shaped by nineteenth-century British voices — John Ruskin, William Morris, F. D. Maurice, and others. This circle (once described by Charles Taylor as "our Victorian contemporaries") was loosely associated with the Pre-Raphaelite Brotherhood; but more importantly, these characters appear as part of the milieu of a vibrant Christian socialism in Victorian England. One can see a constellation of them in Ford Madox Brown's famous painting, *Work,* which hangs in the Manchester City Art Gallery — a piece with F. D. Maurice lurking on the right side of the painting, and with a notice on the left side about classes at the Working Men's College, a project that was near to the heart of William Morris.

Concerned about the effects of the industrial revolution as evidenced in the urban squalor of the working poor, Ruskin, Maurice, and Morris heard the call to love our neighbors not as a dreamy ideal of caring for souls. Rather, they heard this as a clarion call to care for the "whole neighbor," as it were — to be concerned with all the gritty messiness of their embodied reality. While Morris tended toward a utopianism, Ruskin and Maurice were part of a movement concerned with urban renewal. And they realized that loving the neighbor required attention to the material conditions that the neighbor inhabited. This engendered a sweeping movement of social reform especially in northern and industrial England, in cities like Manchester and Liverpool (which is why it is so fitting that Brown's *Work* hangs in the Manchester Gallery, which is free and available to all). This story is chronicled with both detail and verve in Tristram Hunt's book, *Building Jerusalem: The Rise and Fall of the Victorian City.*

These Victorian voices invite us to extend their intuitions: If the call to love the neighbor includes a holistic call to be concerned about the material conditions that the neighbor inhabits, could it also include a call to think about the way in which the built environment itself fosters such concern? In other words, could it be the case that there might be architectural elements that actually mitigate concern for the neighbor, and in fact propagate a kind of egoistic self-interest that blinds us to the neighbor? Conversely, could there be elements of an architecture that foster concern for the neighbor — a mode of design and planning our spaces that regularly and persistently invites us out of ourselves and our involutional worlds of self-interest, and exposes us to the needs of the other?

While I have no interest in espousing some kind of architectural determinism, it does seem to me that our desires and our imaginations — our loves — are shaped in significant ways by the rhythms of our habits and practices. And these rhythms are channeled and molded by the shape of our built environment. A construction of the world that has us sequestered in insulated pods — emerging only into smaller, mobile, insulated pods — has to have an impact on how we see ourselves and our relations to (largely invisible) others. Could there not be a link between the increased narcissism and polarity of North American culture and the fact that many adults spend two hours a day, by themselves, in maddening commuter traffic, with the inanities of talk radio as a soundtrack? Wouldn't we expect this to seep into and shape the imagination in all sorts of deleterious ways?

Conversely, what if our built environment was less sequestering and insulated? What if we dwelt in houses with front porches near the sidewalk — and actually spent time there, chatting with neighbors who stroll by? What if we began our day not jumping alone into the Camry in a dark garage, but by walking a few blocks to catch the bus, which we ride with others, gradually building up familiarity and even friendship with a cross-section of the city we'd never see from inside our automobiles? It seems to me that we'd then be inhabiting a built environment that gives the neighbor a chance to appear. And fostering such environments would be a way to love our neighbors. Disciples of Jesus could commit themselves to an architecture of altruism as a way of loving God.

Loving our neighbor means more than mustering kind feelings toward anonymous others. It might require, here and now, that we commit ourselves to building (or better, recovering and redeeming) built environments in which neighbors actually show up to be loved.

Schools of Faith: On the University

Chapter 7
ARE STUDENTS "CONSUMERS"?

I HAVE BEEN STRUCK by a considerable up-tick in the number of references to students as "consumers" at my home institution, Calvin College, particularly since this nomenclature has been adopted by key leaders in the college community. Granted, a consumerist model of education has been steadily colonizing American higher education over the past decade. What concerns me is the adoption of this paradigm at Calvin College.

Why should the creeping ubiquity of the "student-as-consumer" model mean that Calvin is somehow constrained to adopt this model? Doesn't Calvin College mark itself as distinct precisely because we intentionally resist regnant paradigms in higher education — particularly the reigning orthodoxies of secularism and pragmatism?

And so this essay is an invitation to conversation, not an opening salvo in a "debate." I would simply like to invite the community to consider why Calvin College ought to intentionally resist a consumerist paradigm of education. Indeed, the very project of a liberal arts education runs counter to this "marketization" of education. (If we find ourselves trying to "sell" the liberal arts as a way to land a job and be "successful," we've already sold the farm. We've turned the liberal arts into an instrument of market success.)

So I would like to urge caution about adopting the student-as-consumer model. Let me offer just three themes for consideration.

"Are Students Consumers?" *Chimes* [Calvin College Student Newspaper] (October 20, 2006). Reprinted with permission.

ACQUISITION IS NOT CONSUMPTION

It has been suggested that naming students as "consumers" is just recognizing a fact: that students come to Calvin College to "get" something, to acquire wisdom and knowledge, to come to "possess" skills, and so forth. According to this line of reasoning, to be human is to be a consumer. We need to eat, clothe ourselves, and acquire shelter. To be is to consume.

But this is not the "fact" it purports to be. It is certainly true that being a creature entails being dependent, and thus having to acquire basic goods for human flourishing — including the "goods" of wisdom, knowledge, and know-how. But naming such acquiring as "consuming" is to construe such acquisition in a particular way. Consumption, we might say, is a particular interpretation of "getting," and one that treats the goods and resources of creation as things that exist for *my* interests and happiness. So "consuming" is a particular *way* of acquiring, but not one that is essential. More specifically, to think of our acquisition of goods just as baldly "consuming" is to construe our relationship to the world in a particular way. And I would suggest that construing our relationship to the world as one of "consumption" is to take a good, creational reality of dependence and the need for acquisition in a direction that runs against the grain of God's universe. In sum, consumption is a way of relating to the resources of the world that runs counter to *shalom.*

But what's wrong with understanding our acquisition as "consumption"? Why claim that consuming runs counter to *shalom?* Because understanding our acts of acquisition (whether eating or learning) as "consumption" means we end up construing the resources of creation (whether apples or algebra) as "commodities" there for our "consumption." We thus treat everything as commodities. If consumption is a particular interpretation of "getting," then "commodity" is a particular interpretation of goods. "Consumption" is a way of relating to creational goods such as food and education as if they were things there for the taking. And this way of construing the world of goods reinforces an egocentric way of looking at the world, as if all these things were there *for me,* and for me to do with them what I please. And so the consumer becomes master of the universe: construing the world as a big buffet of things there just for me, I place myself at the center of this universe. My *wants* become the criterion for determining what's important and what's not. *I* get to determine what's on my plate. This reinforces notions of the self as autonomous — a model of the self that runs deeply counter to the Christian tradition, and has long been a special object of critique in the Reformed tradition.

A consumerist relation to goods also comes loaded with the treatment of everything as *disposable* — a view that can be traced back to John Locke's view of property as that which I can dispose of. (See, philosophy does matter!) Consumerism lives off this disposability. For instance, I know you just got a RAZR phone six months ago; but you *need* to chuck that and get the "new and improved" KRZR. In the consumption model, acquisition becomes directed to the self. While it is true that, as creatures, we need to acquire goods in order to flourish, that acquisition is properly for the sake of other ends — ultimately, for the sake of loving God and neighbor. But "consumerism" trains us to treat goods as commodities that are primarily about my happiness.

Understanding ourselves as consumers is not just a simple recognition of the fact that being human requires acquisition. It is a particular way of construing our relation to things as commodities meant to satisfy our wants, easily disposed of when they no longer satisfy. So while it is true that being human means that we need to "acquire" all sorts of goods in order to flourish, it is not just "a fact" that to be human is to be a "consumer." In fact, I would suggest that seeing humans as consumers runs counter to a proper creational understanding of our dependence. The same would be true when it comes to seeing students as essentially consumers.

FORMATION, NOT CONSUMPTION

This leads to a second point. I have just suggested that a consumerist paradigm ends up making an idol of the self as the center of the universe, and thus construes all of the world's "goods" (both the fruits of nature and culture) as if they were there *for me*. To think of education in this way is a recipe for disaster. It reinforces an egocentric attitude in students expressed in the maxim, "The customer is always right." If students are consumers, then they're customers. And a lifetime spent at the mall has taught them that the world is there to provide for their wants, and that the world is populated with people who are there to serve those wants. ("Can I help you find what you're looking for?" the Hollister cashier asks.) It's not surprising, then, that students bring the same consumerist mentality to the classroom. If students are customers, then professors should be more like Gap employees — there to serve the wants of the student.

But the scandal of a liberal arts education is that it's not about giving people what they want.[1] It's about challenging the wants themselves, and ultimately to form and direct those wants and desires otherwise. My task is to invite students to radically reconsider their wants. The professor's task is not to politely and meekly ask, "Can I help you find what you're looking for?" Rather, I want to challenge students by asking: "Why would you be looking for *that?*" A liberal arts education — and especially a *Christian* liberal arts education — should come as a shock to those whose habits have been shaped by a culture of consumerism. This is because the liberal arts are about the *formation* of students, and the central task of formation runs deeply counter to the egocentric stance fostered by consumerism. The very notion of "formation" calls into question the autonomy at the heart of consumerism.

---

1. Someone might respond: "Well, Mr. Professor, there won't be any students in your class to challenge if we don't go out and 'market' Calvin, promote its unique 'brand,' and put some butts in the desks. And you only get to write this kind of reactionary critique of marketing because *we've* done the work marketing Calvin, which pays your bills." I would suggest two related points in reply: (1) Nothing I'm saying here means that Calvin should not *promote* what we're doing far and wide. What I'm suggesting is that "promotion" of Calvin should not be considered as *de facto* a matter of "selling" or "marketing" Calvin to students *as* "consumers." That, Dooyeweerd would suggest, signals an "absolutization of the economic aspect." (2) I'm not even opposed to "marketing" *as such,* but rather the regnant paradigm which construes marketing as essentially marketing-to-consumers. For an alternative consideration of a "reformed" marketing, see Todd Steen and Steve Vanderveen, "Will There Be Marketing in Heaven?" *Perspectives* (November 2003), available at http://www.perspectivesjournal.org/2003/11/essay-marketing.html. However, I would add one proviso: Steen and Vanderveen suggest a kind of "chastened" or tamed consumerism. I would recommend a stewardly understanding of acquisition and reject the conceptuality of "consumerism" altogether. But I think their proposal has a degree of nuance not often seen in these discussions, which tend to just baptize "consuming" as a matter of (creational) fact.

So Calvin College can't have it both ways: we can't talk about "Christian formation" out of one side of our mouth and then play up students as "consumers" out of the other. A distinctively Christian liberal arts education is about the formation of people as a way of resisting consumerism (as a misdirected, fallen way of being "acquiring animals"). Our model here is the medieval university, not the contemporary corporation. We should be looking to monastic Oxford, not corporate Target.

THE "LEADING FUNCTION" OF A COLLEGE

A final theme to consider is the unique vocation of an educational institution. Herman Dooyeweerd, a philosopher in the Reformational tradition, helpfully articulated an understanding of cultural institutions as involving a number of different "aspects."[2] So every institution — whether a college, a hospital, a business, a church, etc. — has an economic aspect, an ethical aspect, a physical aspect, an educational aspect, a faith aspect, and so forth. For instance, while we primarily think of a church's "faith" aspect (its religious function), a church also has to deal with the physical aspect (taking care of its building), the economic aspect (paying its bills and its staff, giving to the poor), the educational aspect (Sunday school teachers), and so forth. A hospital, we might say, is organized around a "biological" aspect, but it, too, has to tend to the economic, physical, etc. You get the idea.

Now, Dooyeweerd also suggested that while each institution involves *all* of the aspects, every institution is defined by a *leading* aspect or function — that aspect *for which* the institution exists and which directs and orients its activities. The leading aspect of a business corporation, for instance, would be an economic aspect — which need not mean that it's all about profit, but that it is primarily focused on commerce and

---

2. See Herman Dooyeweerd, *A New Critique of Theoretical Thought,* trans. David H. Freeman and William S. Young (Philadelphia: Presbyterian and Reformed, 1953-58), Vol. 3, Part II; for a more succinct articulation, see Dooyeweerd, *A Christian Theory of Social Institutions,* trans. Magnus Verbrugge, ed. John Witte Jr. (La Jolla, CA: Dooyeweerd Foundation, 1986), pp. 64-107.

exchange, and all of its activities are oriented by that leading aspect. So the corporation tends to its physical plant in order to carry out its economic tasks well. Again, I think you get the idea.

So, the question is: What is the "leading function" of a university or college? Clearly, the university exists as an *educational* institution: teaching, learning, and research are its core, defining tasks. But, like any cultural institution, the college must also tend to the other aspects: the physical (Physical Plant, IT), the economic (Financial Aid, Business Office, Alumni Relations, grants and giving), the social (Student Life), etc.

Now, Dooyeweerd would contend that an institution is out of whack (that's not the technical Dutch term!) when one of its secondary aspects trumps the leading aspect. For instance, if a hospital becomes *primarily* motivated by profit, it will fail to be the kind of institution it is called to be. Or if a museum existed primarily for the sake of its gift shop, this would represent a certain distortion of the institution. So the question is: does the paradigm of student-as-consumer indicate that the college is unwittingly letting a secondary, economic aspect trump our leading aspect of education, formation, and research? If we start construing education itself in marketing terms, we will end up deforming the institution. And if we let a market-driven notion of "brand" constitute our identity as a college, we will be furthering the disorder of the college as an *educational* institution. (Just as "consumption" is a particular interpretation of "acquiring," and just as "commodity" is a particular interpretation of goods, so "brand" is a particular interpretation of identity.)

I have become more and more convinced that Calvin College needs to recover a sense of its "leading function," and then permit that leading function to position and direct the other aspects of the college. While affirming the holism of a Calvin education, we also need to appreciate the leading function of the institution as one driven by teaching, learning, and research. I want to suggest that this translates into a very concrete principle: it is the academic division of the college that is its animating core, and other divisions of the college (e.g., Admissions, External Relations, Student Life) ought to be oriented, directed, and governed by the academic division. If Calvin College is going to continue to pride itself on being a "faculty-governed" institution, then this faculty-governance should extend to the *entirety* of the college. As currently embodied, we don't have a faculty-governed *college,* we have a faculty-governed academic division. If Calvin is going to be defined by its leading function, this should find expression in its governance and direction, which should mean that other divisions are governed by this primarily *academic* calling. This should mean that the external "image" of the college should grow out of — and be subject to — the academic division, not independently invented by a marketing office, ratified by cabinet, then merely disseminated to faculty.

While students are here to acquire habits, skills, and wisdom, this does not make them "consumers" or customers. As an institution focused on the task of education, we are not providing a "commodity." And having a unique identity does not just translate into being a "brand." In fact, the task of a distinctively Christian liberal arts education is to create a community of people formed to resist and challenge the reductionism of a market-driven culture. To the extent that we do that, we will be faithful to our calling.

Chapter 8
WHY CHRISTIANITY IS SEXIER
THAN LIBERAL DEMOCRACY

JACKIE TAO (in his article "Sexetera") has provided a clear, "realistic,"
and "rational" account of the "simple reality" of sexual freedom. The
argument begins from the "democratic" assumption that "it is one's
right and freedom to choose when to have sex." Further, Tao describes the
adolescent fulfillment of these sexual desires as "normal" and "natural."
After all, "we have to be realistic about ourselves and our capacities," and
certainly "we should not condemn those who" satisfy them. So Tao has
provided a classic American liberal defense for sexual freedom (including
adultery, if he follows his logic), beginning from a notion of individual
rights and freedoms. In the end, Tao's most fundamental commitments
are to liberal democracy: "the most important thing is that they should
be free to make their choice." It's *my* body, Tao seems to protest. And
the Calvin community, if it is going to be "rational" and "democratic," is
called to recognize this.

The problem, however, is that Calvin — despite all of the ways it has
been co-opted by American liberalism — is *not* a democratic, public
community. This is a confessional community whose first confession is
precisely that "I am *not* my own." In fact, more specifically, the tradition
begins with the foundational confession that even my *body* belongs "to
my faithful Savior Jesus Christ" (*Heidelberg Catechism,* Q/A 1). Of course,

---

This piece originally appeared in *Chimes* (February 21, 2003) and was written in
response to an earlier article by Jackie Tao ("Sexetera") which framed the context of
this essay. Reprinted with permission.

Tao is *free* to disagree with this founding confession, just as Calvin as a community is free to reject Tao's religious commitment to individualist democracy; after all, some of the founding documents of his religion are a little old, written to different audiences, and are subject to all kinds of different interpretations (space does not permit me to address Tao's unnuanced criticisms of scriptural authority). Let's just not pretend that the one response is "rational" while the other oppressive. It is not a matter of choosing between authority and freedom, but choosing to *which* authority we will submit ourselves. It is not a matter of choosing between religion and freedom. It is simply a matter of choosing *which* religion: individualist democracy or historic Christianity?

In addition to pointing out the *religious* character of Tao's position, and thus putting both his view and the historic Christian position on at least equal footing, I would briefly supplement this by reminding us of the very *positive* account of sexuality informed by the Scriptures and Christian tradition.

You've probably heard the joke: Why can't Baptists have sex standing up? Because it might lead to dancing! But as a Reformed and charismatic Christian, I believe that dance is to be affirmed as a creational gift of a good Creator. I'll let you draw the conclusion. . . .

What do I mean to suggest by this? My experience in ministry, particularly with youth groups and twenty-somethings, has led me to conclude that too many of our churches lack a positive theology of sexuality. I think this stems from the fact that we have adopted a version of "Platonism" (forgive me, I'm a philosopher). In other words, Protestant fundamentalism has adopted a view of the world and our bodies that resembles Plato's view of the body as an evil prison for good souls. As such, all of the phenomena connected with bodies — like dancing and sex — are understood as basically evil by association. As a result, the only theology of sexuality that young people get in our churches is a negative one: *Don't do it!* This negative theology can become so infectious that it even spills over into marriage. Having been formed by this Platonic/fundamentalist theology, I spent my first year of marital bliss still thinking sex was somehow wrong. (As my four children tangibly demonstrate, I've been cured of my Platonism!)

But this Platonic or fundamentalist account is *not* a biblical under-standing of the human person. When we begin from a theology that affirms the goodness of creation, that entails affirming the goodness of *bodies,* and all the aspects of embodiment associated with it — like danc-ing and sex. However, all of these "goods" of creation fit within a certain "order" of creation. Stanley Hauerwas, drawing on Mennonite theologian John Howard Yoder, has recently given us a rich metaphor that I think helpfully describes this Reformed emphasis on the "order of creation." Hauerwas speaks about "the grain of the universe"; by this he means to suggest that creation has a kind of "grain" to it, just as oak or maple has a distinctive grain, or a putting green has a certain "grain." When we try to go against the grain, we run into terrible difficulties — it does not work well. But if we recognize the grain, and move *with* the grain, things are much easier. What would this mean for a Christian account of sexuality? Sexuality is part of the "grain" of the universe — a wonderful, important part of a good creation. And when this gift is received, welcomed, and celebrated *with* the grain of the universe, we will find wonder-full expe-riences of joy and shalom. But when the gift is *mis*-used — when we go against the grain — we will experience frustration, disappointment, and hurt. The "laws" which Tao rejects are in fact guardrails which are meant to guide us into the experience of joy and protect us from the pain of going against that grain. This is why John's first letter reminds us that God's commandments are not burdensome or oppressive (1 John 5:3).

Let me conclude with just one other affirmation: Reformed Christi-anity is at root catholic Christianity, which is at root a religion of *grace.* Some of us will, at times, have gone against the grain of the universe and experienced the guilt that engenders. Tao wants to free us from guilt by removing the guardrails and pretending there is no "grain" to the universe. But the Christian tradition offers a different way of dealing with that guilt, one that runs *with* the grain of the universe: the Creator's forgiveness, accomplished in and by the God who became flesh for our sakes (John 1:14) and is acquainted with our temptations (Heb. 4:15-16).

According to Tao, young people at Calvin have only two choices: "either to live completely under the strict law or to rebel against it and be morally rejected." This is a fallacious suggestion that ignores the fact that within the logic of Christian faith we need not accept either of his alternatives. On the one hand, we can receive both sexuality and "the law" as gifts of a good Creator. And while living "with the grain of the universe" is by no means easy (I'm not *that* old to have forgotten how difficult it is!), it can nevertheless be joyously pursued as an act of discipleship and formation. In this respect, I think Tao's account is ultimately pessimistic, since it seems to think that temptations and desires cannot be undone, only satisfied or internalized. But Christian faith offers a radical alternative: the very transformation of our character and desires through formation by Word and sacrament.

On the other hand, even when we fail (and we must confess that it is a *failure*), we are not "morally rejected": we are invited by the One who can "sympathize with our weaknesses" to "draw near with confidence to the throne of grace, that we may receive mercy and may find grace to help in time of need" (Heb. 4:15-16).

Chapter 9

BETWEEN THE UNIVERSITY AND THE CHURCH: THE PRECARIOUS (AND PROMISING) SITE OF CAMPUS MINISTRY

I SOMETIMES THINK CAMPUS ministers have a lot in common with the replicants of Ridley Scott's *Blade Runner.* Both occupy a kind of "in-between" place that can generate identity crisis. The replicants, you will recall, are beings who inhabit a kind of grey space between human and machine, and thus can be defined as neither. As they begin to realize this (as in the case of Rachael or Roy), it precipitates deep anxiety about just who they are — and what they're called to be. In a similar way, I think campus ministers occupy such a site — between the university and the church — which can engender salutary questions about the identity and vocation of each.

It is just these kinds of questions that are pursued in John Valk's recent article, "Academically Missional." Contrary to many who see our postmodern climate as though it were the dark post-apocalyptic world of *Blade Runner,* Valk rightly sees the current epoch as one of opportunity for Christian witness in the university. And this signals an opportunity for campus ministers to integrate faith into the center of the university, rather than leaving it as an extra-curricular endeavor — or what Rorty would call a "private" affair that's nice for weekends. (In this way, I see Valk calling for a corrective to the tendencies of parachurch campus ministry described in Paul Bramadat's recent book on Inter-Varsity Christian Fellowship at

"Between the University and the Church: The Precarious (and Promising) Site of Campus Ministry," *Anastasis* [Christian Reformed Campus Ministry Association] 1.2 (2002): 3-4. Reprinted with permission.

McMaster, *The Church on the World's Turf: An Evangelical Christian Group at a Secular University* [Oxford, 2000]. I will return to this important — and contested — qualifier of "parachurch" below.)

However, as Valk himself notes, this raises important questions about the identity and vocation of the campus minister. Questions, of course, are a good thing — they jolt us out of our naïveté and routines and get us thinking about what really matters. I think Valk formulates the right questions — questions with which campus ministers, Christian scholars, and students should all grapple. But in this brief response I would like to reconsider a couple of Valk's answers, doing so in the spirit of "carrying on the conversation." (In what follows, I will assume, like Valk, that we are largely talking about campus ministry on a public, "secular" campus such as a Dalhousie or UBC. I think the discussion of campus ministries on other kinds of campuses — such as Catholic universities or Christian liberal arts colleges — warrants attention. Further, we could ask whether one must be at a public or secular university in order to be "academically missional." But I will not address these questions here.)

Let me first return to the situation of "in-betweenness" that confronts campus ministers. Campus ministry occupies a unique site *between* the church and the university. I use "church" in a strong sense here — in the vein of John Howard Yoder or Stanley Hauerwas — to denote a community of faith formed by tradition and engaged in worship of the Triune God. The fact that campus ministers (and campus ministry) — such as Christian Reformed Church chaplains — are between the *church* and the university creates the possibility for what I think is a needed corrective of much that goes under the rubric of "the integration of faith and learning." Let me explain. Too often, the rhetoric of "integrating faith and learning" trades on a very thin notion of "faith" and tends to generate a very individual-istic (and modernist) paradigm: I, the lone ranger Christian scholar, am trying to integrate *my* particular faith commitments into my scholarly work (which, for the record, also largely happens in isolation — there are more closed doors than open ones in our academic departments). Unfortunately, I think much parachurch campus ministry — which tends to represent "Christianity" rather than the church — feeds into this in a couple of ways: (1) we can end up reducing "the faith" that gets integrated into a very intellectualized commodity ("ideas") and/or (2) we end up making the liturgy and worship life of the church marginal or optional at best, unnecessary at worst. What's curious to me is the way in which the latter — removing the church from any integral role in Christian scholarship — can be the product of either very emotivist, subjectivist evangelical versions of Christianity (the "bad side" of the charismatic tradition) or of very intellectualist versions (the "bad side" of the Reformed tradition).

So I am very interested in the role that a particular kind of campus minister and campus ministry can play: those who are commissioned as "ambassadors" — such as CRC chaplains — not merely of a "faith," but a *church.* I think campus ministers can play a unique role by reminding students and scholars alike that *the church* plays a role in the "redemption of knowledge" and the formation of Christian scholars (whether students or professors). And this should be demonstrated in the worship life sponsored by these ministries. On this model, both the lectures and the liturgy are at the center, and central to the vocation of campus ministry. If Christian scholarship is a matter of "bringing every thought captive," it demands what Linda Zagzebski describes as "virtues of the mind." So Christian scholarship demands *formation,* and the most important site of such formation is the worship life of the church. As such, campus ministry occupies this "between" place and is in fact called to be the church *for* the university.

Now, because I would advocate this model (we might call it the "campus ministry as *polis*" model — stealing a line from Hauerwas), I have a couple of reservations about Valk's concrete proposals. First, I do not share his concern about "proselytizing." Valk, while advocating Christian voices in the classroom, concedes that "the classroom in a public university is not a place to proselytize." Of course, on one level, I understand that it is not the site for an evangelistic crusade (no danger of CRC chaplains staging one of those!). On the other hand, it is important to let the secular university see that it is always already engaged in proselytization and give it a dose of its own medicine. I think the presence of campus ministry in the academy will be at its best when it is kerygmatic, not apologetic.

Second, I think Valk's suggestion regarding the role of campus ministers in the classroom indicates a bit of "replicant-like" ambiguity regarding the vocation of the campus minister. Specifically, he suggests that "[m]aybe campus ministers can be catalysts in and for a new way. Perhaps the time has come for campus ministry to carve out new space in the university — a place in the classroom, a place at the center of the academy. And where the opportunities exist, perhaps campus ministry can even partner with the university, to be purposefully in the classroom." Now, some of my best friends are replicants — er, campus ministers — and they do in fact have a voice in the classroom at universities. But they have earned that hearing, I think, not by virtue of being campus ministers, but by being (Christian) *scholars*. Of course, the two are not mutually exclusive; but the fact that the two can be combined in one person does not mean we shouldn't distinguish two different vocations. I'm not interested in any kind of turf war, but isn't what Valk is calling for — a Christian voice in the university classroom — the calling of Christian *professors?* Valk's proposal raises good questions, however. Just what is the relationship — and difference — between campus ministers (many of whom have PhDs) and Christian professors? Are they competing for the same piece of academic turf? On the model I've painted above, I think the campus minister serves a prophetic function, reminding the Christian professor and scholar of the essential role of the *church* in the development of a Christian mind — and nourishing such through both the organization of worship and liturgy as well as creating space for Christian theoretical reflection. Of course, some campus ministers will have the added opportunity of serving as adjunct faculty at the university, but that seems to me a different role.

Further, Valk's hope that campus ministers could make it into the "center" of the academy — the classroom — may be a bit premature. Despite the current postmodern condition and critique of the "myth of neutrality," the public, secular university remains very much a *modern* institution, committed to ideals of "objectivity." If there are any "postmoderns" at the university, they're assistant professors in the English Department; provosts and academic vice presidents, on the other hand, remain very much committed to an Enlightenment notion of a pure, objective, universal Truth. And even those "postmoderns" who are to be found in our universities are wont to recognize the *religious* character of their presuppositions and commitments. So there are strict limits to the modern university's pluralism: a multiplicity of perspectives, commitments, and worldviews is encouraged *so long as* those commitments are not religious, and above all, not Christian. Those Christian scholars who do make it into the center do so either by making sacrifices others might consider too costly (vis-à-vis the confessional or constructive Christian character of their work), or by doing "stealth" Christian scholarship which operates under the modern university's radar, so to speak.

How should we confront this persistent modernity of the university? With lectures, panels, debates, roundtables, and group discussions to be sure; but also with the proclamation of the gospel in the worship of the church — a liturgical proclamation which forms Christian students and scholars as agents of redemption. One of the primary intellectual goals of campus ministry should be to remind the university of its ultimately religious character. As such, campus ministers can find an ally in postmodern discourse which criticizes the university's continuing pretensions to being an objective arbiter of Truth. In this way, Valk is absolutely right to find in postmodernity a space carved out for religious discourse at the center — yea, heart — of the university. As Jacques Derrida concludes his *Memoirs of the Blind,* an extended meditation on the conditions of knowledge: *"Je ne sais pas; il faut croire."* I don't know; one has to believe. That is the first profession of every professor, whether they recognize it or not; and so it is the founding confession of the university, even if the institution tries to act otherwise. In short, one of the aspects of campus ministry should be to remind the university that it is always already a community of commitment.

But coupled with this (negative) apologetic goal should be a (constructive) kerygmatic discourse and liturgical life which demonstrates an alternative community of commitment. Like replicants, campus ministers — and all those involved in campus ministry — are a "peculiar people," called to the discipleship of mind.

Chapter 10
SCHOOLS OF THOUGHT; OR, WHY
THE STATE SHOULDN'T FUND MBAs

AMERICAN LAW AND politics remain governed by the antiquated notion of secularity. Consider the U.S. Supreme Court's decision in *Locke v. Davey,* which ruled that the state of Washington's Promise Scholarship Program could legitimately exclude funding for those pursuing "a devotional theology degree." (A similar exclusion in Michigan is currently being challenged in federal court.) Though registered at an accredited college, Joshua Davey was denied the Promise Scholarship, which he earned on the basis of both merit and need, because he was training for the ministry. While recognizing the Establishment Clause of the First Amendment, Davey argued that tax-based funding of training for religious vocation could avoid the state's endorsement of religion without compromising the Free Exercise Clause.

Commentators, including Linda Greenhouse in the *New York Times,* have already suggested that this decision spells the end of all kinds of programs from kindergarten to college. But we should avoid the alarmist response already evidenced in Justice Scalia's dissenting opinion, which worried about slippery slopes. The decision in *Locke v. Davey* is quite narrow and focused. The court did *not* rule against state funds supporting students who pursue education at "pervasively religious institutions." Indeed, the college that Davey attended — Northwest College in Kirk-

"Schools of Thought," in *Sightings,* published by the Martin Marty Center at the University of Chicago, June 14, 2004. Reprinted with permission.

land, Washington — is a denominational college of the Assemblies of God, where all students are required to take courses in Bible, "Spiritual Development," Evangelism, and "Christian Doctrine." But the state of Washington did not exclude participation in the Promise program for students at Northwest or other religious colleges *so long as* their course of study was aimed at a "secular" profession.

This question of profession and vocation is at the heart of the court's decision. In Justice Rehnquist's majority opinion, the issue is not religion *per se,* but more specifically "training for religious professions." In other words, Washington's state constitution does not unjustly exclude education and instruction in religious institutions, or even curricula and degrees which include required courses in "devotional theology"; rather, the state's elucidation of the Establishment Clause "has merely chosen not to fund a distinct category of instruction," namely, degrees intended for professional religious vocation. Rehnquist appeals to a long history of worries about tax dollars paying for pastors.

Here's where the court's decision gets interesting. The fundamental assumption informing the judgment is the claim that "training for religious professions and training for secular professions are not fungible." The majority opinion suggests that religion is so unique that "professional" religious vocations "find no counterpart with respect to other callings or professions."

While I accept the interests of the Establishment Clause, it seems to me that the court's decision is a bit naive about the distinction between sacred and secular, between "religious" and other vocations. The majority opinion marks out degrees in "devotional theology" because they are designed to induce a particular faith. But isn't there a sense in which a business degree is also intended to induce a particular faith (in the market)? Isn't there something quite indoctrinating about many of the programs in business at state universities, which function as a kind of novitiate, orienting students to a set of doctrines and a new worldview? Indeed, one could suggest that much that goes under the banner of "secular" education is, in fact, a kind of religious formation where students are initiated into a particular worldview — a set of commitments that govern how they see the world and act within it. As Thomas Kuhn put it, even in the objective world of the sciences, what counts as "normal science" is really a kind of orthodoxy.

What the court's decision fails to question is the very idea of the "secular." It assumes that the secular is neutral and non-religious, whereas in fact the secular commitments of the market and political liberalism constitute a *different* religion. As such, the very notion of the secular is a kind of modern hangover in our postmodern world. In postmodernity, there is no secular, because there is no neutrality. Every vocation is religious in a formal sense of being committed to a particular worldview. So the supposedly radical distinction between religious and other secular vocations breaks down when we reject the very notion of the secular.

And here's the irony: Joshua Davey was a double major in pastoral ministries and business management/administration. The state of Washington denied his Promise Scholarship because his pastoral ministries degree was religious. But was his business management degree really much different? If the state will not give tax dollars to M.Div. students, should it not also refuse to fund MBA degrees?

Chapter 11

A COMMENCEMENT, A WEDDING, AND AN ALTERNATIVE POLITICS

AS THE PRESIDENT of the United States delivered the commencement address at my institutional home, Calvin College, I was celebrating a wedding with a young couple whom my wife and I counseled during their engagement. Being on sabbatical excused me from attending, so I chose the wedding over the President's visit. Because of this, I was confronted with questions on two fronts.

To astonished West Michiganders (while Michigan was colored a blue state in the 2000 election, it's western environs are a deep rouge), I had to admit that I was going to pass on this wonderful "honor" to be in the presence of the President. But to many of my equally disappointed colleagues, I also had to explain why I wasn't there to wear an armband at the ceremony, and why I didn't sign the faculty's letter of protest, which received national media attention. It was the latter group I found to be less charitable, calling into question my commitment to the vaulted Niebuhrian dream of "transforming culture." One colleague even dug up the Reformed tradition's oldest and vilest epithet, suggesting that I was acting like (gasp!) an "Anabaptist."

But being at the wedding, I want to suggest, was a *political* act. (Of course, it was also a good time; but not *that* good: it was a Baptist wedding, so *sans* libations.)

Let me backtrack a bit: as most now know, in 2004 our campus was

---

This piece began its life on my public commentary blog, Fors Clavigera.

shaken from its West Michigan Republican slumber with the announcement that our commencement address would be delivered by the President of the United States. Almost immediately, all kinds of coalitions of dissent and protest began to form. Eventually amongst the faculty two dominant modes of engagement won out: a plan to wear symbolic armbands during the commencement, and an opportunity to sign an "open letter" to President Bush, articulating a critique of his own policies and a more constructive vision of politics seeking justice for all.

And then it slowly began to happen: the unfolding of a *Seinfeld* episode. You know the one: where Kramer participates in the AIDS walk but prefers not to wear a red ribbon. As a result, he finds himself accosted by an angry group of ribbon-wearing activists.

"What!?" is the response. "*Who* won't wear the ribbon? Why won't you wear the ribbon? You're against AIDS, aren't you? Then why won't you wear the ribbon?" Kramer collapses under the blows of other protesters.

I began to experience something similar: "Why won't you sign the letter? Aren't you opposed to Bush's policies?" Yes, absolutely, was my reply; but I also wasn't comfortable with the articulation of an alternative which still, to my mind, was trying to play the game by the rules of a politics that wasn't mine.

For instance, I couldn't sign on to the criticism of the Iraq war as "unjust" and "unjustified" because the letter, while purporting to speak from Christian confession, entertained that war *could* be just, which I don't. So, with a sense of respect for those undertaking this organized dissent, I politely declined participation, sent our RSVP to the wedding, and began to check the couple's gift registry.

While I was prepared for brusque treatment from those on the right, I wasn't really prepared for the hegemonic response from my "progressive" sisters and brothers. Because of my (non)response — which they variously labeled as quietest, pietist, escapist, perfectionist, purist, Anabaptist, and sectarian — a number of my colleagues judged that I was either a cop-out or a sell-out. One was even happy to label my "silence" as *evil*. If you won't wear the ribbon, if you won't sign the letter, if you won't wear the armband, you must be complicit with the system. By not signing the letter, I might as well have pushed the button on the cruise missiles that tragically shattered an Iraqi family's wedding.

Being called evil is a bit hard to take — especially for someone who has been an outspoken critic of the war in Iraq (and war in general), as well as the injustices that are the fruit of capitalist systems for distributing resources, not to mention the maddening conflation of foreign policy with bastardized theology. But because I didn't respond in the "right way," because I wasn't "participating in the political process," I was remaining silent — silently evil.

Once I gathered my thoughts, however, I responded with a question: Why would you conclude that because I'm not signing your letter that I'm being "silent"? Is there only one way to speak? If I don't do what *you're* doing, does that mean I'm not doing anything?

A proper response in this situation must proceed from a careful diagnosis. And it is here that I think my progressive colleagues are a bit shortsighted. We need to first ask: Why was it that so many in Calvin's constituency — and many other Christians in West Michigan — eagerly welcomed President Bush into a central ritual of our college community? Why is it that the Reformed cultural elite have come to so closely identify being faithful with being committed to a party that privileges the wealthy, is aggressively militaristic, and caters to the *nouveau riche* of late capitalism?

My answer would be both simple and complex: this represents *a failure of discipleship*. If we find the climate of highly churched West Michigan to be so complicit with institutionalized social injustice, then we have no one to blame but ourselves. Clearly, our churches, far from forming us otherwise, are actually contributing to the formation of docile subjects of the GOP machine.

What, then, would be a fitting response? Armbands? A letter?

If the problem is a failure of discipleship, the only proper response must be a rigorous commitment to re-imagining Christian formation. The best response will be a matter of worship, not publicity. (And, in fact, I fear the "open letter" to President Bush only exacerbated the problem, galvanizing the constituency and confirming all their suspicions about "liberal" academics.)

So we went to the wedding. We participated in a liturgy of worship that, to some degree, had the goal of constituting a "peculiar people" whose politics is otherwise. And what I'll continue "doing" is try to reshape and reeducate the imagination of the church so that in time church members will be formed as disciples who will immediately see the injustice of exploitive domestic policies and the utter inconsistency between Christian confession and militaristic foreign policy. I guess I'm taking a longer term view (which doesn't play well with activist urgency). I'm also taking a stance of hopeful charity, trusting the possibility that the Spirit can change hearts and minds — even in West Michigan! (Such a miracle would be enough to make the staunchest Reformed folk entertain Pentecostal visions.)

And here I must confess that I don't see many of my progressive sisters and brothers eager or willing to take up this hard, long work of disciple-ship and formation in the churches. Many of my colleagues who so loudly and publicly protested the Bush visit with their armbands and other dec-larations tend to inhabit ecclesial spaces where they'll find many sympa-thetic to their political stance — and from there articulate their prophetic critique. But as Richard Mouw wisely counseled me several months ago, we need fewer prophets, and more teachers. Or as Klaas Schilder put it a half-century ago, in his own little book on *Christ and Culture* penned in the shadow of fascism:

> Blessed is my *wise* ward-elder who does his home visiting in the right way. He is a *cultural* force, although he may not be aware of it. Let them mock him: they do not know what they are doing, those cultural gadabouts of the other side!

So I'll continue to see my adult Sunday school class and our Bible study group — even my college classroom — as *political* spaces where, slowly to be sure, disciples of Jesus are shaped by the politics of Jesus. This politics doesn't play the game of party lines or state power, but rather seeks to form us otherwise — as those who desire a different kingdom and who serve a king-in-waiting.

Chapter 12
LOST IN TRANSLATION?
ON THE SECULARIZATION OF THE FALL

THERE WAS A TIME in the mid-1990s when Christian theorists commonly referred to Derrida, Foucault, and their ilk as perceptive observers of the fallenness of the world. Granted, Paris was no Lourdes: one wouldn't look to them for healing. But one could find in these "postmodern" theories — focused on power and violence — a solid diagnosis of the human condition as experienced in a broken, post-lapsarian world. Indeed, Heidegger, Derrida, Foucault, and others were read as if they were good Calvinists with a highly calibrated sensitivity to all the ways humanity is prone to perversion, domination, and sin. In the same vein, Merold Westphal pointed out the way in which the masters of suspicion — Nietzsche, Marx, and Freud — could be read almost as Puritans of a sort, discerning humanity's ubiquitous predilection for idolatries of all kinds.[1]

1. Merold Westphal, *Suspicion and Faith: The Religious Uses of Modern Atheism* (Grand Rapids: Eerdmans, 1993). This kind of project is helpfully extended in Bruce Ellis Benson, *Graven Ideologies: Nietzsche, Derrida and Marion on Modern Idolatry* (Downers Grove, IL: InterVarsity Press, 2002), which provides something of a supplement to Westphal. I offered a specific account of Heidegger's reworking of the doctrine of the Fall and a myth of fallenness in Derrida in *The Fall of Interpretation: Philosophical Foundations for a Creational Hermeneutic* (Downers Grove, IL: InterVarsity, 2000), ch. 3. And John Milbank considers the way in which Christian theologemes are taken up and reworked in modern social theory in *Theology and Social Theory* (Oxford: Blackwell, 1990). One could argue that the recent work of Alain Badiou and Slavoj Zizek on Saint Paul translates not the Fall, but redemption, into a formal philosophical notion.

"Lost in Translation? On the Secularization of the Fall," *Books & Culture* 13.6 (November/December, 2007): 36. Reprinted with permission.

So phenomenology and post-structuralism were considered new renditions of a story as old as Augustine (or Moses, depending on one's account of doctrinal development): a tale of original sin.

Such readings are not fantastic feats of eisegesis or merely the inventions of Christian scholars looking to underwrite their interest in continental theory. In other words, these often aren't just matters of convergence, but influence — sometimes direct, in other cases more oblique. In some instances, there are paper trails that point us to the specifically Christian origins of what emerged as "secular" theory. Take, for example, Heidegger's landmark work *Being and Time* (published in 1927). Upon its publication, Rudolf Bultmann thought he had discovered gold in Marburg. Undertaking what can only be described as a monumental work of apologetics, Bultmann had been trying to show that the existential core of the New Testament's teaching could be affirmed as true because it was corroborated by the neutral, philosophical work of Heidegger's *Being and Time*. O happy coincidence! thought Bultmann. The New Testament understanding of the human condition could be demonstrated as true through the secular philosophical confirmation of this vision of the human condition unveiled by Heidegger's hermeneutic phenomenology. But as the later publication of Heidegger's early lectures has shown, this was not merely a happy coincidence: the "secular" vision of the human condition in *Being and Time* did not constitute independent evidence for the New Testament. In fact, there was no independence at all: Heidegger had first worked out the basic themes of *Being and Time* by lecturing on Saint Augustine and Paul's letters to the Thessalonians! What emerged from his hut in the Black Forest was not the independent verification of the New Testament that Bultmann's apologetic project required; rather, *Being and Time* was a sort of translation or "formalization" of the Pauline vision (such that Bultmann's project was akin to translating the King James Version back into Greek).

For readers attuned to these conversations, Stephen Mulhall's *Philosophical Myths of the Fall* will be neither surprising nor counterintuitive. But we should not therefore underestimate the element of scandal in Mulhall's project, which is to suggest that key canonical figures in modern philosophy — Nietzsche, Heidegger, and Wittgenstein — re-perform the Christian doctrine of original sin. As Mulhall puts it, "all three in fact engender a conception of the human condition that constantly inclines them to reiterate elements of a distinctively Christian structure of thought" (p. 13). The result is a "secularized conception of the self and its world" (p. 11) — a translation or formalization of the particularities of Christian confession into more neutral or more universal categories, and thus unhitched from any specific faith commitments.

Mulhall is absolutely right to see this project of secularizing or formalizing Christian theological resources at work in Nietzsche, Heidegger, and Wittgenstein — just as others have discerned something of the same in Marx, Freud, and Derrida. Indeed, Mulhall's essays offer unique contributions to these discussions by patiently and carefully showing the way in which Nietzsche repeats his own myth of a "Fall," or the way in which Wittgenstein's *Philosophical Investigations* could be plausibly read as a re-performance of Augustine's *Confessions.* And he does all this in the crisp lucidity that is produced by the rare chemical reaction that occurs when one mixes the analytic rigor of Oxford with the continental labyrinths of Nietzsche and Heidegger's prose.

But these secular translations engender two related problems that deserve consideration. First, just *what* is getting translated? What's taken to be the Christian story that is then reworked and secularized? And second, what happens to the Christian story in that process? Is there something lost in translation? Or as Mulhall asks, "can one say what the Christian has to say about the human condition as fallen, and yet mean it otherwise?" (p. 13).

On the first score, Mulhall falls into just the trap that Nietzsche, Heidegger, and Wittgenstein do: conflating fallenness with finitude. In other words, the so-called Christian doctrine that is put on the table to be "translated" turns out to be not received catholic orthodoxy, but already some bastardization of the church's confession. In this case, Mulhall persistently takes it that the doctrine of original sin specifies that human desire is sinfully perverted "by virtue of their very condition as human" (p. 6). In a favorite turn of phrase Mulhall repeatedly emphasizes that humans are "always already" errant, corrupted, and misdirected. To be human, then, is to be "essentially" sinful (p. 105), "sinful simply by virtue of being human" (p. 38; cp. p. 118). Sin is considered to be part of the very fabric and "structure" of being human (p. 119).

But that is decidedly *not* the orthodox doctrine of original sin but rather an all-too-common gnostic rendition of it (one to which, admittedly, evangelical Protestants are sometimes prone). This is to read the Bible as if it began with the third chapter of Genesis. The paradox is that a proper understanding of original sin does not posit sin as properly "original"; that is, it does not attribute sinfulness, perversion, and errancy as being coincident with being human and finite. A doctrine of original sin minus the prior affirmation of the goodness of creation is not the catholic doctrine of the Fall; it is rather a gnostic perversion of the doctrine that posits sin *as* original, as essential to and coincident with being human. And when such a misunderstanding of original sin is coupled with some hope of redemption, we find the contorted philosophical acrobatics that Mulhall finds in Heidegger and Wittgenstein: redemption from this condition of fallenness requires redemption from being human. So humanity is seen as originally and essentially perverted, but overcoming this situation requires going against the very "nature" that is seen to be original. In other words, the essential fallenness of humanity is anti-human; but at the same time, given that this is part of the structure of being human, redemption would also be anti-human. As Mulhall comments, "Dasein's nature is such that it bars its own way to what belongs most properly to that nature" (p. 56). A strange world, indeed. But this incongruity should not be confused with the mystery of the Christian vision, but rather the tortured perplexity of a gnostic worldview.

What is consistently lacking in these secularized or formalized versions of the Fall is the distinct nuance of the Christian vision, namely, the ability to imagine the world otherwise. The doctrine of creation is precisely that: an assertion that our present condition is "not the way it's supposed to be," as Cornelius Plantinga so aptly put it. So, too, the doctrine of the eschaton, which enables the Christian story to imagine humanity remaining finite and human but inhabiting the world otherwise. This is why Abraham Kuyper suggested that Christian scientists and scholars would always be "abnormalists," not tempted to confuse our currently observable world with the way things ought to be. To confess with the creed that God is the "maker of heaven and earth" and conclude our confession with the hope of "the resurrection of the dead" is to be able to imagine humanity otherwise while still affirming the finitude and embodiment that are constitutive of being creatures.

What guides Mulhall's reading — and here he's just being faithful to his subjects — is a doctrine of the Fall without Creation (the book tellingly opens with Genesis 3 as an epigraph). But the orthodox doctrine is clear: without the prior goodness of creation, there is no Fall. So what gets "translated" in these projects is not the doctrine of original sin. Rather, what we get is an "ontologizing" of the Fall, an inscription of fallenness into the very structure and fabric of being human. Creation is always already a Fall; creation and Fall are coincident. But is this ontologizing of the Fall the same as a secular "translation" of the Fall? Is the ontologizing of the Fall merely a "formalization" of the Christian doctrine into formal, secular terms? Or is there something lost in translation, such that the language of fallenness is now used to describe a very different phenomenon?

This raises the second question: what happens to Christian doctrine when it is formalized or secularized in this way? What gets lost in translation? As already noted, these translation projects seem prone to start with something other than the properly orthodox understandings of Christian doctrine. But even more, the translation projects of a Heidegger or a Wittgenstein are undertaken precisely in order to purge the specificity of Christian confession from the doctrines in order to distill a universal, supposedly neutral account of "the human condition" — to tell us that this is "just the way it is." Their goal is to "unchain" the myth of the Fall from the specificities of Christian faith — and a persistent line in Mulhall's book is to call into question the extent (and even the possibility) of their success in this regard, considering the ways in which these formalizations or secularizations of Christian doctrine fail to completely detach themselves from the specificity of Christian faith. Thus Mulhall, in somewhat Rahnerian fashion, seems to hint that Nietzsche, Heidegger, and Wittgenstein are closet Christians of a sort, precisely because their philosophical myths of the Fall can't completely unhook themselves from their theological origin.

But there is also a second trajectory of concern that Mulhall doesn't seem to consider: that is the way in which these secularization projects yield not "translations," but something different altogether — that despite similar tropes, a very different story is being told. And here I think Christian theorists need to be especially discerning: because the rhythms and rhymes of Heidegger and Derrida can *sound* like secular renditions of the Christian story, we can be lulled into something like Bultmann's euphoria, thinking that continental philosophy has "got religion" and now bolsters our Christian claims about the human condition. But it's precisely when Heidegger or Derrida or Badiou takes up themes from the Christian story that we should more carefully consider just what's getting said in and through these re-deployed theological terms. Mulhall's survey should help us to appreciate the way in which contemporary philosophy is wont to draw on the spiritual capital of Christian theologemes but deny the power thereof. When that happens, what matters most is lost in translation.

Faith in America: On Politics and the Church

Chapter 13

CHRISTIAN WORSHIP
AS PUBLIC DISTURBANCE

One day, as we were going to the place of prayer, we met a slave-girl who had a spirit of divination and brought her owners a great deal of money by fortune-telling. While she followed Paul and us, she would cry out, "These men are slaves of the Most High God, who proclaim to you a way of salvation." She kept doing this for many days. But Paul, very much annoyed, turned and said to the spirit, "I order you in the name of Jesus Christ to come out of her." And it came out that very hour.

But when her owners saw that their hope of making money was gone, they seized Paul and Silas and dragged them into the market-place before the authorities. When they had brought them before the magistrates, they said, "These men are disturbing our city; they are Jews and are advocating customs that are not lawful for us as Romans to adopt or observe." The crowd joined in attacking them, and the magistrates had them stripped of their clothing and ordered them to be beaten with rods. After they had given them a severe flogging, they threw them into prison and ordered the jailer to keep them securely. Following these instructions, he put them in the innermost cell and fastened their feet in the stocks.

About midnight Paul and Silas were praying and singing hymns to God, and the prisoners were listening to them. Suddenly there was an

"Christian Worship as Public Disturbance: Acting as Ambassadors of a King-in-Waiting," *Minds in the Making,* An e-Collection from Calvin College (Volume 1, Issue 2). Reprinted with permission.

earthquake, so violent that the foundations of the prison were shaken; and immediately all the doors were opened and everyone's chains were unfastened.

Acts 16:16-26

AMBASSADORS OF THE KING

When you read the book of Acts, it's hard not to notice a pattern: that when the gospel is preached, it causes a public disturbance. Whole cities are thrown into riots by the message proclaimed by the apostles. In fact, when Paul's presence in Thessalonica brought more civil unrest, people protested to the authorities that "these men who have upset the whole world have come here also" (Acts 17:6).

But when we read passages like this, they seem so distant from our experience as to be unbelievable. When was the last time the city of Grand Rapids was thrown into public chaos because of a worship service? And yet, in Acts 16, here is a whole city — the realms of both commerce and government — so threatened by these disciples of Jesus that they subject them to torture and imprisonment. We are so far from experiencing that kind of treatment that we have to come up with some explanation of why it happened to the first Christians and not to us.

The answer we give ourselves is that the apostles were living in a very different culture — a society that was hostile to the gospel. So the reason they were treated differently is because the society they inhabited was so opposed to the gospel. We, on the other hand, enjoy living in a democracy — the land of the free — and so enjoy a culture that is, by and large, friendly to the gospel. Sure, there are tensions, but we are not beaten and tortured for proclaiming Christ because we live in a very different world, a different time.

Or could it be that we're preaching a different gospel? If our proclamation of Christ does not upset the powers-that-be — if it doesn't "turn the world upside down" (Acts 17:6) — is that because our culture is friendly to the gospel? Or have we made the gospel friendly to our culture? If we aren't treated like Paul, is that because society has changed — or have *we* changed? Could it be that we preach a gospel that gives no occasion for the powers-that-be to be concerned or threatened? Have we, in fact, changed our story in such a way that the gospel we preach pledges allegiance to these powers?

Before we think about those questions in light of Scripture, I want to recall a scene from *The Return of the King.* Arriving in Minas Tirith, Gandalf approaches the one sitting upon the throne with a kind of subversive respect: "Hail Denethor, son of Ecthelion, Lord and Steward of Gondor." Denethor, Gandalf reminds him, is a *steward* of the throne, but not its rightful king. The fact is not lost on Denethor, who perceives Gandalf's presence as a threat to his power and dominion. "Do you think the eyes of the white tower are blind?" Denethor asks. "I have seen more than you know. With your left hand you would use me as a shield against Mordor. And with the right you seek to supplant me. I know who rides with Theoden of Rohan. Oh yes, the word has reached my ears of this Aragorn son of Arathorn. And I tell you now, I will not bow to this Ranger from the North, last of a ragged house, long bereft of lordship." The steward of Gondor understands very clearly who Gandalf represents: he is an ambassador of the rightful king (Aragorn). And as such, Gandalf represents a king who threatens Denethor's demand for allegiance. Thus Gandalf will never be a docile subject of Denethor; rather, he is a subversive. And his departing words remind Denethor of just this fact: "Authority is not given you to deny the return of the king, *Steward.*"

This encounter, I think, can help us to understand why the apostles were subjected to torture and imprisonment by the powers-that-be: they were ambassadors of a rival king, acting contrary to the decrees of Caesar precisely because they had pledged allegiance to another king (Acts 17:7). The gospel that Paul preached was *politically* subversive. As N. T. Wright summarizes, Paul's "missionary work must be conceived not simply in terms of a traveling evangelist offering people a new religious experience, but of an ambassador for a king-in-waiting, establishing cells of people loyal to this new king, and ordering their lives according to his story, his symbols."[1] The gospel, then, is deeply *counterimperial* — against the

---

1. N. T. Wright, "Paul's Gospel and Caesar's Empire," in *Paul and Politics: Ekklesia, Israel, Imperium, Interpretation,* ed. Richard A. Horsley (Harrisburg, PA: Trinity Press International, 2000), pp. 161-62.

empires of the Caesars of our world. If our proclamation and practice do not elicit these kinds of reactions from the powers-that-be, is it perhaps because the gospel we preach is no longer subversive — because we have compromised our allegiance to the King of kings? I invite you to consider the model of the apostles' counterimperial practice as a paradigm for the nature of Christian worship and practice.

Now, let me anticipate an initial response: "Well, Jamie," someone will say, "the big difference is that in those days — of Rome and Caesar, in an era of empire — 'religion' and 'politics' were intertwined. Caesar demanded not just obedience, but worship; not just taxes, but sacrifice. But that's not the case today: politics and religion are distinct. We don't have a king or emperor, we have a President. And he certainly doesn't claim to be divine or demand our worship."

Well, that may be the case. But that does not mean that the political and economic empires of our day don't command absolute allegiance. This blending of politics and religious fervor hit home for me in a supermarket checkout aisle in the fall of 2001. Usually lined with candy bars and tabloids, the checkout line was now bounded by a book display. Rows of hardcover texts were wrapped in a red-white-and-blue cover with writing emblazoned on them. As I inched closer, I could see that these books were in fact "Holy Bibles," and the writing inscribed on the cover was a quotation from Psalm 33:12: "Blessed is the nation whose God is the Lord." We might think that in our culture, religion and politics are more distinct. But consider the rhetoric we hear about making the ultimate sacrifice for one's country, the shape of patriotism and allegiance, and the temples that dot Washington, D.C. Just because we don't (officially) deify the President doesn't mean that "America" isn't a kind of empire which demands our allegiance. (If you don't think so, try *not* standing for the national anthem at the next ballgame you attend. See what happens.)

So maybe Paul's context and our own is not that different. Maybe like those original apostles, we also live in the shadow of empires: political, economic, media, and so forth. Then why doesn't our proclamation of Christ engender the kind of public disturbance we see here in Acts 16? Let's consider this passage from Acts with new eyes attuned to both Paul's political context and our own.

DISTURBING THE PEACE

Note three key aspects of the story here: the *context,* the *content* of their witness, and the *confrontation* it caused.

Note where this takes place (v. 12): in Philippi, "a Roman colony." This is crucial for understanding what follows. A Roman colony was like a piece of Rome transplanted abroad: an outpost of the empire in a faraway place. Philippi was made a colony after being "rescued" by the emperor, Augustus Octavian, in 31 B.C. The citizens of Philippi, then, were actually citizens of Rome — enjoying the same privileges and benefits, as well as paying the same tribute to the emperor, whom they hailed as a "savior." At the time that Paul is in Philippi, Rome's emperor cult was in full swing. In fact, the term "gospel" *(euangelion)* meant "the celebration of the accession, or birth, of a king or emperor." So in the Roman colony of Philippi, the main gospel that would be heard would be that proclaiming Caesar as savior, anointed one, and Lord *(kyrios).*[2]

Ironically, the content of the Christians' witness is summarized in the words of a possessed young woman: "These men are servants of the Most High God, who are proclaiming to you the way of salvation" (v. 17). In Rome, or an outpost of Rome like Philippi, this would be immediately heard as a challenge. Our most high is Caesar, they would say; our savior is the emperor.

So what happens? The city rises up against Paul and Silas, but the cause of their distress is complex. Clearly, they see Paul and Silas as a threat; or better, they perceive the King whom they represent to be a threat. But to what? Well, to two things really: to commerce and to empire — a threat to the marketplace and a threat to the public space of politics. It's important for us to see this complicity between the market and the empire — a complicity that is only intensified today. Granted, the instigators of unrest — like those later in Ephesus (Acts 19:23-27) — primarily see their own *profits* being threatened (Acts 16:19). But they appeal to the authorities on the basis of the fact that the gospel of Paul represents political subversion, for he proclaims an allegiance to another King — other than Caesar.

2. Wright, "Paul's Gospel and Caesar's Empire," pp. 165-66.

The gospel that Paul preached was not a message about some private, interior transformation of the heart. It was a message about a new allegiance to a King-in-waiting. As such, there was something radically *political* about the gospel — which didn't mean, of course, that Christians sided with a particular political party. In fact, there was a sense in which Christians, who pledge allegiance to a resurrected King, could never find themselves at home with *any* party of the empire. The call to discipleship is a call to be formed into the kind of people who pursue a *telos* which is found in Christ. This translates into a way of life that is governed by justice and mercy, not power and the accumulation of goods. Thus first-century cultures recognized that the gospel subverted the interests of the empire and the interests of "the market." There is a sense in which Christians were not very good Romans, not very good participants in idolatrous economies, and so were "bad for business."

With this context in mind, and in light of this confrontation in Philippi, look with new eyes at what Paul wrote in his letter to the Philippians a few years later.

RETHINKING OUR CITIZENSHIP

Some of Paul's key exhortations to the Philippian Christians are lost on us because of poor translations (and lack of appreciation for the colonial context). In Philippians 1:27, one of Paul's first exhortations is for them to "live as *citizens* in a manner worthy of the gospel." In Philippians 3:20, Paul reminds these inhabitants of the Roman colony that, as Christians, "we are citizens of a heavenly commonwealth [*politeuma*]." We are citizens of a different empire. The church of Jesus Christ is an alternative city, a counter-empire. We are the "Messiah-people" who pledge allegiance to the Lamb. We are subjects of a king who tells us to put away our swords. We are a peculiar people, "a royal priesthood and a holy nation" (1 Peter 2:9), whose allegiance transcends the boundaries of *states* and *nations* — making us "strangers" in every nation and state (1 Peter 2:11).

So we need to ask ourselves: just what does it mean to pledge allegiance? What are we doing when we pledge allegiance to a flag, or a particular nation state? What are we doing when, with our time and money, we pledge allegiance to the accumulation of material possessions and consumer products? Can we pledge allegiance to both God and mammon? Can we pledge allegiance to the empire of Jesus and still serve the empires of capitalism and an unfettered market? If I pledge allegiance to the Messiah, how would I support violence which leads to the deaths of my brothers and sisters in other countries? If the city of Grand Rapids hasn't been disturbed by our proclamation of the gospel, is that because G.R. is some of kind New G-R-usalem? Or is it because we've blunted the subversiveness of being allied to Jesus and being subjects of *his* kingdom? Does our allegiance to the King-in-waiting pose a threat to power and wealth?

But what does this have to do with worship? Well, we need to ask ourselves: What is worship *for?* What does worship *do?* While God's glory is the central aspect of worship, its principal effect is the *formation* of the body of Christ into the image of Christ. It is in full-orbed worship (Word and sacrament) that we are formed as subjects of the King. It is in worship that our allegiance is molded and directed to Christ. So Christian worship is the school of the Spirit. But, given what we've learned in Paul's engagements in Philippi, we could also say that Christian worship is a kind of civics class: it is where we are shaped into "Messiah-people," who pledge allegiance to the ascended King-in-waiting, and learn the counter-imperial measures of love, justice, and mercy. The goal of worship is not a private re-fueling, but a public disturbance — to create subversive ambassadors of the coming King.

Chapter 14

HOW TO GET YOUR HANDS DIRTY

I N HER CONTRIBUTION to *Anxious about Empire* (May 2005), Jean Bethke Elshtain scolds those Christians not willing to get their hands "dirty" by compromising, for instance, a Christian commitment to peace and nonviolence. On her account, Christians who criticize the Iraq war, or war in general, aren't willing to deal with the "reality" of being citizens engaged in "this world." But I've heard the virtue of "dirty hands" extolled by "progressive" Christians on the left as well, particularly against those with (apparently "clean-handed") Anabaptist tendencies who center their account of politics in the worship and discipleship of the church.

This is a common refrain, especially from Reformed folk who've been hooked by the Niebuhrian thrill of "transforming culture." But I continue to be nonplussed, and I find this refrain assumes an either/or dichotomy which is a tad simplistic.

Is there only one way to get your hands dirty? Ironically, this "dirty hands" rhetoric is employed by both right and left. On the one hand, our conservative brothers and sisters on the Religious Right try to convince us that in the name of "liberty" — which is a "gift from God" — we need to be willing to get our hands dirty and undertake military action. On the other hand, "progressive," *Sojourners*-type activists disparage the ecclesial-centric politics of Stanley Hauerwas and others as "purist" and "quietist" — as if committing to the church as *polis* was a way of staying

---

"How to Get Your Hands Dirty," *Perspectives: A Journal of Reformed Thought,* June/July 2005. Reprinted with permission.

"clean." On the matter of "dirty hands," I think Jim Wallis and NAE President Ted Haggard are on the same continuum: both think that getting one's hands dirty means getting into bed with the state. (I won't run with the metaphor.)

But is pulling a trigger the only way to get your hands dirty? Is playing by the rules of party (and partisan) politics, even liberal democracy, the only way to really care about justice? Is that the only way to "do" something about oppression and injustice? Aren't pacifists who minister to the wounded and open up their sanctuaries tending to victims also getting their hands dirty? Could we not say that those who celebrate the Eucharist *as* politics also have mud and blood on their hands?

One can see this powerfully pictured in Roland Joffé's film *The Mission*. According to the "dirty hands" logic, Rodrigo must appear as the hero who, fighting for justice, is willing to take up arms and "get his hands dirty." Satisfying activist urgency, at least Rodrigo *does* something.

While Rodrigo undertakes his military response, Father Gabriel responds with what, from the "dirty hands" perspective, must be judged an escapist, quietist strategy: he embraces women and children, celebrates the Eucharist, and dies in a hail of gunfire while carrying the Host. Didn't the blood and mud also dirty Father Gabriel's hands? Isn't the celebration of the Eucharist a *doing* which testifies to a kingdom that is coming? Is not this *doing* a witness that invites the world to imagine itself otherwise?

What I find telling is the concluding sequence of the film: when combing through the remains of the village, the children who survive don't pick up the weapons lying next to Rodrigo and other rebels. Instead, they retrieve the violin — the music brought to them by Father Gabriel. If the gospel is a song of peace, it seems that Father Gabriel's dirty hands not only *did* something, but did something more powerful than Rodrigo's sword.

Chapter 15

GOD, THE FUTURE, AND THE POLITICS OF FREEDOM: REFLECTIONS ON "OPEN THEISM"

MY OLDEST SON has developed an interesting defense mechanism. If we are at a restaurant and his three younger siblings start acting up with quite embarrassing routines, Grayson has a brilliant way of creating some healthy distance: "Thank you, Mr. and Mrs. Smith, for inviting me to dinner," he retorts, quite audibly, hoping neighboring families won't think he's one of "us." It's his sly little survival strategy, a way of trying to say, "I'm not really a member of this crazy family."

I'm sometimes tempted by a similar strategy when it comes to my evangelical family. Electoral politics provides no shortage of such cases, but as an academic, a more recent case-in-point hits home: As reported in the *Century,* Huntington College (soon to be — ironically? — Huntington *University*) will not renew the contract of John Sanders, a noted and controversial proponent of "open theism." Already in 2003, the board of the college, acting on behalf of the Church of the United Brethren in Christ which controls the college, removed Sanders from the tenure track, not just because of his stance on open theism, but apparently because of his very public role in such debates, and because of his position training future ministers in Bible and theology. (William Hasker, an emeritus professor of philosophy at Huntington College, is also a proponent of

---

"What God Knows: The Debate on 'Open Theism,'" *Christian Century,* June 12, 2005, pp. 30-32. Reprinted with permission.

open theism but has never been censured by the college. Huntington president G. Blair Dowden notes this is because Hasker was "not teaching theology or Bible.")

Sanders's struggles at Huntington came on the heels of a nasty debate within the Evangelical Theological Society over the past several years. Led by Roger Nicole, a significant faction within the ETS wanted to see Sanders and Clark Pinnock (another proponent of open theism) expelled from the society on the grounds that their position with respect to God's foreknowledge was inconsistent with the ETS doctrinal standard of inerrancy. Ultimately, after a vote by the ETS membership, both Sanders and Pinnock were permitted to remain members of the society, though 62.7 percent voted to oust Sanders. Being allowed to remain in the ETS must have felt a bit like being "permitted" to live in a home where you're not wanted.

Granted, vitriolic rhetoric in the service of truth is a bit of an evangelical forte. (I have letters at home from former professors describing me as a "student of Judas Iscariot" who had turned to "another Gospel" — and this all because I dared to agree with Gadamer!) Those on the outside, who (are fortunate enough to) use the word "evangelical" only in the third person, won't find it at all surprising to hear of such harsh policing of theological boundaries and lack of interest in academic freedom. "I do believe that the right to publish and academic freedom statements that the professors actually are working under are being violated," Sanders told *Christianity Today.* "They are being trodden upon." Dowden offered a response that, in fact, gets to the heart of the debate. While academic freedom is important, he said, it is not absolute: "For all Christian colleges, academic freedom is bounded in some way." I would suggest that at the heart of this debate is a question about how we understand freedom theologically — and how we understand academic freedom is predicated on a *theology* of freedom (see William Cavanaugh's contribution to *Conflicting Allegiances*). And our theology of freedom, I want to suggest, carries both political baggage and political import.

Just what is at stake in this debate regarding "open theism"? And why has this elicited such passionate opposition in evangelical circles? Is this just more biblicist scholasticism? Or is there something at stake here that warrants our interest?

Let's first get a handle on open theism: What are its key elements? What concerns does it seek to address? On this score, it is important to emphasize a deeply pastoral impetus behind the development of open theism. For noted openness theologians such as Sanders and Gregory Boyd, the founding moment of open theism is the pastoral challenge of evil and suffering. Sanders opens *The God Who Risks* by recounting the tragic death of his brother, and Boyd closes *God of the Possible* with an extensive treatment of the pastoral implications of open theism in the face of tragedy. As such, open theism is a response to a long-standing challenge for Christian confession: If God is all-powerful, perfectly good, and has complete knowledge of the future, how could God permit the evil and suffering we see on both global and personal levels? If God knew that such suffering would occur, the open theist reasons, then there must be some sense in which God is responsible for such evil, which would compromise God's goodness. Since such a conclusion would be clearly contrary to Scripture and the Christian theological tradition, the open theist offers another account: God didn't know.

Open theism, then, is a retooling of our understanding of God's fore-knowledge. However, reactionary critics notwithstanding, it must be immediately noted that open theism does not reject God's omniscience. Boyd states this very clearly: "The issue is not whether God's knowledge is perfect. It is. The issue is about the nature of the reality that God perfectly knows" (*God of the Possible,* p. 16). At issue, then, is not how much God knows, but what there is to be known. In particular, the question concerns what we might call the "ontological status" of the future: is "the future" some*thing* that exists to be known? More specifically, can the future actions of free moral agents be known before such free decisions are made? Open theism contends that God cannot know the future of free moral agents, not because of some lack in God's knowledge or power or cognitive ability, but because the future of such free agents does not exist as an object to be known. God does not know the sufferings that a dictator will inflict upon his people, not because God's power to know is impoverished, but simply because what such a free agent will do in the future is open, and therefore does not exist to be known. The future is blank and only filled in after choices are made.

But one can anticipate an objection: if God's knowledge entails knowing that such evil and suffering is at least *possible,* then why create the world? Why create a world of free moral agents if one of the possible outcomes is a world of domestic abuse and genocide? At the heart of the openness view of God is a picture of God as a *risk taker.* For God the creator, evil and suffering are necessary risks that attend the creation of a world of free moral agents who can relate to God in love. Unlike process theologians, open theists continue to assert creation *ex nihilo* (indeed, one of the curious theoretical lines of investigation here is the tension in open theism between maintaining creation *ex nihilo* and asserting the more process-like notion that God is somehow "dependent upon" and "conditioned by" creation). Creation, then, is not a necessary emanation that God "needs" to be complete; rather, creation is gratuitous and primarily *out of* love and *for* love. God freely decided to create beings who were capable of loving relationships, but the necessary condition of such love was freedom. And the necessary risk of such freedom was evil. Evil and suffering, then, were contingent future possibilities, but precisely insofar as they were the effects of decisions made by free moral agents, they were part of a "future" that did not exist. In other words, they did not "exist" to be known, even by God. There are thus limits to God's foreknowledge; but these limits are not internal to God, but rather stem from the nature of what there "is" to be known.

We should note that, despite the rantings of Roger Nicole, Bruce Ware, and others, open theism does seem clearly within the purview of orthodoxy. Indeed, the utter biblicism of open theists makes it a uniquely evangelical phenomenon, stemming from an engagement with Scripture that seeks to be sincere and honest, even if it's a bit naïve in thinking that one comes to the Scriptures without a host of philosophical assumptions. (A common strategy of open theists is to denounce "classical" notions of sovereignty as the product of the "Hellenization" of scriptural exegesis, whereas Sanders and others seem to think that they are coming to Scripture without metaphysical commitments. Curious is the fact that the "Hellenization" thesis was once the province of the quintessentially liberal theology of Harnack & Co.) Since open theists explicitly affirm creation *ex nihilo* and even God's omniscience, it is hard to see how one could conclude that open theism is heretical. The most animated opponents of open theism take themselves to be defending God against assault, whereas it is more likely that they are anxious about defending certain boundaries of identity. (One could undertake a certain psychoanalytic read of the situation at this point, but we must forgo that for sake of space.)

However, this revisioning of God's foreknowledge, like a stone dropped into a pond, has ripple effects across the theological spectrum, raising challenging questions about the nature of divine providence and sovereignty, prophecy, and prayer, just to mention a few. One can understand why such a radical rethinking with such broad implications would generate intense debate, particularly for the evangelical communities which value faithfulness to Scripture and theological orthodoxy. In this respect, I must confess that it is almost refreshing to have a battle amongst evangelicals that isn't about drums and guitars in worship. Here is a debate that is quite forthrightly theological; indeed, it seems that what is at stake is nothing less than our beliefs about the nature of God. That, one might think, is something worth fighting about. However, upon closer analysis we will find that what really drives open theism is not a conception of God, but, more importantly, a certain understanding of human freedom. Theologically, it also raises important questions about language and the possibility of speaking about God. And finally, I want to suggest that there is a curious politics submerged beneath this debate.

One of our first reactions might be to write off the whole debate as archaic and, worse yet, downright "scholastic" — a favorite epithet hurled against the backward by the "enlightened." But I want to suggest that there can be some virtue to such supposedly scholastic discussions. Indeed, I have found that parishioners are sometimes more interested in "scholastic" questions than theologians. Indeed, "scholastic" questions are precisely those awkward, difficult questions put to us by nine-year-olds. I recall teaching at an inner-city Pentecostal church where young people were intensely interested in questions about prayer and God's foreknowledge as matters important to their discipleship. So when theologians are quick to dismiss a debate as "scholastic" (by which they variously mean irrelevant or conservative), I think we ought to operate with a hermeneutics of charity that strives to hear "the sense of the faithful" emerging from such discussions. With respect to open theism, I think we are laudably pushed to consider several important themes: the nature of confessional language, some important theological questions about human freedom, and perhaps ultimately even some *political* questions about freedom.

Just what are we doing when we confess that God is good? Or beautiful? Or sovereign? Or what are we to make of the Scriptures that describe God as repenting or changing his mind? Open theism pushes us to reconsider the way religious language works. Our classical conceptions of God have tended to downplay certain ways of talking about God as "merely" metaphorical. So when Scripture speaks about God "repenting" or changing in some respect, the classical tradition has suggested that such language, as metaphorical, does not properly describe God's essence; whereas when Scripture asserts that God does not change, such language is taken to properly describe God's essence. When God is described "anthropomorphically" — described as having human traits or characteristics — this has been downplayed as metaphor, which was shorthand for saying this wasn't *really* the case. Open theists, in contrast, take such metaphorical language seriously. Indeed, there might even be something postliberal about open theism insofar as it seeks to let the language of Scripture be that which governs the imagination (though it also remains plagued by the postliberal naïveté concerning the possibility of stepping outside of metaphysics). If, in the end, I think there is legitimate reason to be concerned that open theism presents a notion of God that is a projection of just the kind of god modernity wants, I nevertheless think that open theism poses very important questions about the nature of scriptural and confessional language.

So the open theism debate raises important questions: Does our language "hook onto" God in some way? Are we really saying something about God in such words? Is God so wholly other that such statements never really reach their target? Is our confessional language ultimately equivocal, with no real connection between what we say and who God is? Or, conversely, is there so little difference between God and creatures that, as Joan Osborne suggests, God is just "one of us"? Is God "good" in the same way that we are good? Is our language about God univocal, such that God is conditioned by a general notion of goodness external to God?

The latter, univocal notion of confessional language would seem to reduce God to little more than an idol: theology, as Feuerbach suggested, would just be anthropology, and all of our talk about God would end up simply talk about ourselves. But the former, equivocal notion of theological language would disconnect us from any real knowledge of God, leaving us within a flattened, quiet realm where confessional language never makes it outside of the atmosphere of immanence. Ironically, then, both univocity and equivocity wind up in the same place, leaving us with religious language that merely bounces around the echo chamber of immanent reality, never being ruptured *by* transcendence or making its way out *to* transcendence.

This is why a long theological tradition, embodied especially in Augustine and Aquinas, has suggested that our confessional language operates on the basis of analogy, refusing the closed heaven of both equivocity and univocity. And both emphasized that the paradigm for understanding this was the Incarnation itself, whereby the transcendent inhabits immanence, really and fully, without giving up transcendence. The Word becoming flesh, piercing that atmospheric ceiling of immanence, is that which underwrites our own words about God. This means that our confessional language both "hooks onto" God *and* is characterized by some slippage. God is given in such language and at the same time exceeds our metaphors. God gives himself to understanding, all the while resisting comprehension. This translates into a confessional confidence that eschews the skeptical agnosticism of post-Kaufmann theologies; but it also translates into a confessional humility which quickly runs up against the limits of religious language. As Saint Augustine once explained it to his parishioners, "We are talking about God; so why are you surprised if you cannot grasp it? I mean, if you can grasp it, it isn't God. Let us rather make a devout confession of ignorance, instead of a brash profession of knowledge" (Sermon 117.5). My evangelical sisters and brothers (well, it's mainly the brothers) would do well to be reminded of such sanctified ignorance when it comes to their confident denouncements of open theism. But we all do well to take seriously this incarnational operation of language. Retrieving a sense of analogy is to confess that "In the beginning was metaphor."

What really drives open theism is a second key theme: the nature of human freedom. It is not unfair, I think, to describe open theism as the logical consequence of an Arminian understanding of human nature, free will, and the effects of sin. Indeed, what open theists have shown is that Arminians who operated with a "classical" (read: Calvinist) understanding of God's foreknowledge were working with a contradictory system. The open theism debate, however, is not just a rehashing of old Arminian-Calvinist debates, largely because open theism just assumes an Arminian understanding of freedom and then seeks to (logically) extend the implications of this to our understanding of God. Open theism is, at root, a theology of freedom, both divine and human. But what exactly does it mean to be "free"?

Open theism, reflecting a common consensus in contemporary philosophy of religion, simply assumes a libertarian notion of human freedom. This is what Isaiah Berlin famously described as a "negative" understanding of freedom: one is free insofar as one is free *from* external constraints. To be free is to be autonomous and self-determining, free to do otherwise. Freedom is freedom of *choice*. It is this understanding of freedom which is enshrined in liberal democracy. This construal of freedom is so deeply ingrained in our culture, and even in contemporary theology and Christian philosophy, that we find it almost impossible to think of freedom in any other way. Open theism, assuming that humans are free in just this way, constructs an account of God's foreknowledge that attempts to reconcile claims about God's omniscience with the inventive possibilities of human freedom — the sense that human choice *creates* the future as it goes. In this sense, open theism sees God as "making room" for human choice by granting space for human autonomy, even if that means God takes the risk that we will choose badly, as we so often do. It is precisely this intuition that makes open theism a constructive, but still orthodox response to the challenge of evil and our confession that God is good.

However, I think it is important to note that another trajectory in the Christian tradition argues that we should not understand freedom in libertarian terms. Augustine, for instance, emphasized a "positive" understanding of freedom as empowerment: I am free insofar as I am able to achieve the good. On this score, freedom isn't just the ability to choose, but the ability to choose well, to choose rightly. What is valued, then, is not autonomy, but rather a healthy sense of dependence upon God — even a participation in God as that which properly orients us to the *telos* that constitutes human flourishing. In this telling of the story, sin and evil result from the very desire to be autonomous, to secure one's independence from God.

Given the complexities of this problem, and the inadequacy of language, we ought to be humble about which approach we take. And we might do well to hold both models in some kind of dialectical tension. That said, I wonder if perhaps some political considerations might tip the scales in this regard. In closing, I want to suggest that we should also be attentive to the political presuppositions that might color our theological understanding, as well as the way our theologies of freedom might translate into some surprising political policies.

In particular, could there be a sense in which open theism's concern for human autonomy reflects an accommodation to the picture of human nature bequeathed to us by modernity, and liberal democracy in particular? Could it be that open theism, like modernity, flirts with idolizing freedom as autonomy?

Recall that open theism developed as a response to suffering and evil, which are understood as the results of God taking a risk. What God wanted was a relationship of love with his creatures, and such a loving relation required freedom as its condition. So the open theist thinks that freedom of choice is a good that warrants suffering. But is this not almost to make freedom of choice an end in itself? Might one not, in the vein of Ivan Karamazov, suggest that creation in that case was a pretty irresponsible risk for God to take? If the price of freedom is the suffering of children, we might conclude that freedom's not worth the price of admission and happily return the ticket.

I can't help but read this theological controversy within the context of our current political climate, where freedom has been enlisted as the engine that drives a hawkish foreign policy, even while it is also employed to guard a *laissez-faire* global economy. President Bush's second inaugural address harnessed the language of freedom as the guiding principle of

America's democratic missionary calling, and regularly linked this to a theological principle that freedom is the "gift of the Almighty" to every human being. But what concept of freedom is at work here? Clearly, the rhetoric of the current administration — which so reveres the ideal of a free market — is predicated on a libertarian or "negative" notion of human freedom, as is the notion of freedom assumed by open theism. (What's strange here is that, on the one hand, open theism openly espouses a libertarian view of human freedom and is castigated as "liberal" by conservative critics. But on the other hand, these same critics, Al Moehler for instance, are often beholden to the most classically liberal notions of freedom in their civic theology.)

The open theism debate could be instructive if it moves to the next level and interrogates this assumption that freedom is *ipso facto* libertarian. For as David Burrell has recently shown (in his book *Faith and Freedom*), not only are such libertarian notions of freedom contrary to a long history of theistic thought, but, more importantly, such a reduction of freedom to choosing plays right into the hands of capitalism's valuing of choice for its own sake, with no concern for *telos* or choosing well. If open theism seeks to resist the static, dispassionate god of an antique metaphysics, has it played into the hands of a market-driven god who is only too happy to multiply choices for the sake of consumption? Is it any wonder, then, that evangelical churches find themselves reduced to marketing "God"?

Rather than dismissing this debate as yet more evangelical bickering or scholastic wrangling, we might look to the open theism controversy as an opportunity to revisit fundamental questions about our confessional language and, more importantly, how to understand "freedom" in an age when liberty is the banner under which a creeping empire expands. It could be that the Son who makes us "free indeed" frees us, above all, from enslavement to libertarian notions of human autonomy, with consequences for both Christian worship and public theology.

Chapter 16

IT ONLY HURTS WHEN I LAUGH:
WHY *HARPER'S* WON'T CHANGE AMERICA

THE MAY (2005) issue of *Harper's* magazine is, as usual, a feast. There is a distinct theme running through this issue, which comprises an almost apocalyptic collection of editorials and essays chronicling the dangers of evangelical Christianity — from Lewis H. Lapham's characteristic fundamentalism of the left, through Jeff Sharlet's foray into the exurban world of Ted Haggard's megachurch, to Chris Hedges's hilarious and frightening tour of the National Religious Broadcasters conference. The writing is crisp and witty, the research is thorough, and the tone sometimes even charitable. This is just the kind of stuff that makes some of us shell out cash for *Harper's, The Atlantic,* and other favorite cultural observers.

But I can't stop thinking about French anthropologist Claude Lévi-Strauss, as periodicals are increasingly publishing pieces that I would call "*Harper's* anthropology" (though you'll also find examples of this type of journalism in *The Atlantic,* the *New York Times,* and other key media outlets). Just as western anthropologists of generations past trudged through island jungles in search of the exotic "other" in "primitive" societies, so today journalists depart from the safety and civilization of Manhattan to the exotic environs of . . . Kansas! — or Oklahoma, or Florida, or Colorado Springs.

Not having seen middle Americans who actually believe in God, these

"It Only Hurts When I Laugh: Why *Harper's* Won't Change America," *Sightings,* published by the Martin Marty Center at the University of Chicago, June 30, 2005. Reprinted with permission.

journalists cum anthropologists are simultaneously awed, bewildered, fascinated, and frightened by what they find. Their articles read a bit like dispatches from strange lands. "I've been to red America," they seem to say, "and it's stranger and scarier than you could have imagined."

One of the letters in the May issue of the magazine astutely observes that this kind of *Harper's* anthropology serves only to exacerbate what is perceived by some to be a problem with (to cite the cliché) "suburban, evangelical America." It is just this tone that contributes to the martyr complex that comfortable, middle-class white folks feel in suburban Kansas City — and it is precisely this sense of victimhood that galvanizes the Religious Right.

Now, I enjoy the sardonic witticisms of *Harper's* anthropologists. And I remain convinced that many of the journalists' observations are right on the money. I get the jokes because I *live* with this stuff. When, for instance, Sharlet describes "Commander Tom"'s maniacal commitment to the Royal Rangers (an Assemblies of God version of the Boy Scouts), I have a weird sense of laughing at myself since I, too, have seen the Frontiersmen Christian Fellowship at Royal Rangers Camperoos. My own sons have worked their way through the ranks of Straight Arrows, Buckaroos, and Trailblazers. And Sharlet is right: there are parts of this organization that are downright spooky. Or when Hedges describes the creepy netherworld of Christian radio, with its holy dieting programs and violent anti-gay rhetoric, he is accurately describing one force significantly shaping the imaginations of many Christians who would describe themselves as "evangelical."

But here's the rub: To someone intimately acquainted with these particular expressions of evangelical Christianity, it is obvious that *Harper's* anthropologists aren't going to change things. Sorties from New York to exotic locales like Colorado Springs will feed the alarmist stance of detached coastal regions, but these dispatches from the twilight zone of the Midwest aren't going to change the hearts and minds that matter. If, as an evangelical, I am disturbed by what I see played out under the banner of the Religious Right, I know that countering this won't be accomplished by witty, derisive editorials in my favorite magazines — not even witty, sympathetic editorials in *Sightings*!

Rather, what it will take is a patient, charitable transformation of the evangelical imagination from the inside. And this can't be done by visitors writing for *Harper's*. It will require a long-term commitment to reeducating evangelical hearts and minds in venues of denominational magazines like *The Pentecostal Evangel* or the Christian Reformed Church *Banner* — and perhaps even the airwaves of — gasp! — Christian radio.

That will be a calling not for visiting anthropologists, but for resident teachers.

Chapter 17
THE ECONOMICS OF
THE EMERGING CHURCH

MAYBE THIS IS a legacy of my blue-collar upbringing. Maybe it's even tinged with a hint of sour grapes. Maybe I'm just plain jealous. But a couple of years ago, I read with some interest *The Quarterlife Crisis* by Alexandra Robbins and Abby Wilner, concerned with "the unique challenge of life in your twenties" (as the subtitle billed it). I hated the book: partly because of its rabid individualism, but more because of its obvious socio-economic location. Story after story went something like this: "After Ashley [*sic!*] graduated from Stanford, she just wasn't sure what to do with her life, so she explored her options by finishing an MBA at Harvard. Now that's come to a completion and she's facing 'the real world.' Sure, it would be fine for her to become the vice-president of her father's multi-million-dollar corporation, but she's looking for more than that. Now she's beset with postmodern *Angst.*"

Yeah, life's a bitch when you're a Stanford grad with a Harvard MBA. What's a poor girl to do?

Recently I've been bothered by a similar socio-economic suspicion regarding the "postmodern" or "emerging church." Don't get me wrong: I understand the program and have some sympathy for the vision that's been sketched by folks like Brian McLaren and Robert Webber. But I have

---

"The Economics of the Emerging Church," *TheOoze* [www.theooze.com], November 14, 2003. Reprinted with permission.

this nagging question: "What's the median income of a 'new kind of Christian'?"

Before trying to grapple with that question, let me try to motivate my concern from another angle. For the last few years, our family were members of an inner-city church in Los Angeles: a community of incredible ethnic and socio-economic diversity with an effective outreach to former gang members from crews like Lennox 13. Since moving to Grand Rapids, we've joined another urban congregation with an intentional focus on diversity, racial reconciliation, and community empowerment (in a very disempowered neighborhood). And our family has chosen to live in the community with hopes of being agents of redemption. What does the emerging church have to say to these communities — with horrible public schools (and so little if any post-secondary education) and families trapped in cycles of disempowerment because of drugs and incarceration? I'm just not sure that my neighbors, or those who live in the vicinity of our church, are asking the question that, up to this point, the emerging church has been trying to answer. They don't subscribe to *Regeneration Quarterly* (and couldn't afford to if they wanted to); and — as a very important indicator of class — many don't have Internet access in their homes. So they're not reading *The Next Wave* or *The Ooze*. While the emerging church wants to be "urban," in my town it largely ministers to the young urban professionals living in the hip new condos downtown on the riverfront. But how can the emerging church reach those folks living on south Division or at Eastern and Franklin — places those people in the condos won't drive after dark?

Even if the people living on south Division could log on to *The Next Wave* or pick up a copy of a pomo magazine, I don't think these outlets would speak to them. These postmodern outlets are asking questions that are largely the province of college-educated middle-class America. That's why I think, in the vein of my earlier question, we need to ask ourselves: How bourgeois is the emerging church? Or better, and with more hope, let's formulate the question this way: What can we do to prevent the emerging church from being simply another bourgeois institution?

Before suggesting how that might be done, I think it's important to appreciate how we got to be where and who we are. There is some sense in which the very posture of *questioning* is a bourgeois privilege. (This is why I constantly remind my students that, while they might not think so, it is a privilege just to be able to sit in a freshman philosophy class and ask the kinds of questions we do. Large segments of the American population never have the chance — let alone vast portions of the global population.) We have the opportunity to think through the kinds of questions that Dan Poole grapples with in *A New Kind of Christian* only after (and because) more fundamental questions — like how to pay the rent, how to keep our children safe, who will pay for groceries — have already been settled. Further, insofar as Poole's questions are occasioned by a prior knowledge, the questions actually follow from a fairly solid, and generally post-secondary, education. If the emerging church is really "postmodern," then it's at least had the chance to be *modern;* or in other words, the "new kind of Christian" sketched by McLaren has had the chance to grapple with skepticism only because she's had the opportunity and privilege to ask the questions. Skepticism is a luxury. In this respect, the new *post*modern kind of Christian is not as different from Descartes — that paragon of *modernity* — as she might think. Indeed, the picture we get of Descartes in his *Meditations* is one of privilege and luxury, for here's a person who can take five or six days just to think about — albeit important — intellectual challenges. That happens only with a healthy endowment, or the patronage of a wealthy prince — and servants taking care of the mundane aspects of survival. The servants, of course, don't get the opportunity to meditate on the possibility of evil deceivers.

So the emerging church has the privilege of being postmodern because it's had the privilege of having been modern. But how will the postmodern church reach those who've been on the underside of modernity? What will the emerging church have to say — or better, what will it have to *ask* — for those who haven't enjoyed the benefits of Descartes' legacy? I would briefly suggest a two-pronged agenda that grows, I think, out of some of the core values of the emerging church.

If one of the key tenets of the emerging church is the centrality of embodied, incarnational witness, then one of the places we need to embody the redemption purchased by Christ on the cross is in the disempowered neighborhoods in our cities. Thus the first part of my suggested program is to merge the concerns of the postmodern church with the concerns of urban renewal; in other words, new kinds of Christians should be passionately concerned with building new kinds of cities — which will mean that they should be passionately concerned with impacting the socio-economic structures that systematically disempower parts of town like south Division. Our cities are largely the production of very modern forces, and their decay is a testimony to the underside of modernity. What could be more postmodern than redeeming these urban spaces and city-dwellers, informed by a vision of the kingdom whose telos is a city (Rev. 21:2)? This project for a new urbanism also resonates with another central tenet of the emerging church: its opposition to "Constantinian" Christianity as civil religion. The economic structures which have created the south Divisions of our country are largely the product of classic American liberal polity, which the church as civic cult has been all too eager to defend. The postmodern, counter-cultural church as witness will find no better space for exercising its alternative vision than in our cities' neighborhoods.

If the first arm of the program I envision is urban, the second arm is global. This is because my concern about the bourgeois character of the emerging church is intricately bound up with its still being what appears to be a largely American, or at least North Atlantic, phenomenon (with important British incarnations which feel a bit different). If the emerging church so far has had little to say on south Division, it's had even less to say to Latin America. Thus I want to suggest that the discussion around the emerging church needs to be globalized by being merged with discussions concerning what Philip Jenkins has described as "the next Christianity." As Jenkins has argued, the axis of the Christian world is quickly shifting to the south. If the postmodern church wants to speak for the church of the twenty-first century, it had better buy a plane ticket — because the church of the next century will find its "new center" not in Colorado Springs, Washington, or even Seattle, but somewhere on the African continent. This doesn't mean that emerging church discussions have nothing to say to global Christianity. On the contrary, I think the post-secular outlook of the emerging church can offer a critical perspective in a global context. But we must see ourselves as *servants to* global Christianity, utilizing our gifts and resources to think *with* our global sisters and brothers rather than coming with pre-packaged answers to "postmodern" questions they've never asked.

Chapter 18

THE PENDULUM OF EVANGELICALS AND POLITICS: ON GREG BOYD'S *MYTH OF A CHRISTIAN NATION*

THE UNFOLDING STORY of evangelicals and politics in America has a certain Hegelian rhythm to it: like a pendulum swinging from one extreme to another, evangelical thinking about politics has swung from a kind of pietist stance of withdrawal and even suspicion to a strident, triumphalist program for "taking America back for God." Greg Boyd's book *The Myth of a Christian Nation* is a sign that the pendulum might be headed back to the other side of its arc.

But before we go further we need to appreciate the story so far. A rough-and-ready rendition might go something like this.

Once upon a time, evangelicals considered their primary mission and calling to be oriented by the Great Commission. What mattered was eternity, and what was urgent was the salvation of souls. And while such evangelistic work was often attended by charity and works of mercy, few evangelicals could justify expending energy on "worldly" tasks such as politics. But in the early 1970s, some important and influential voices began to point out that this understanding of the church's calling was a bit truncated. In particular, emerging voices like Ron Sider and Jim Wallis argued for a more holistic understanding of the gospel, noting the model of Jesus' own ministry which attended to concrete, "worldly" matters of poverty and illness as occasions for redemption (Luke 4:14-20).

"Replacing Rallies with Revivals [on Greg Boyd's *Myth of a Christian Nation*]," *Christianity Today* Online, 5 October 2006. Reprinted with permission.

At the same time Richard Mouw, from a distinctly Reformed per-spective, invited evangelicals to see the dualism of the status quo: that their concern with souls and eternity ignored God's own affirmation of the goodness of bodies and the temporal world. By ignoring the realm of politics and culture, evangelicals were unwittingly giving over these spheres of creation to the forces of distortion and destruction, rather than redemptively redirecting them. By neglecting the tasks of govern-ment, for instance, evangelicals were abandoning wide swaths of God's good creation to the enemy. Thus Mouw invited evangelicals to take up the Cultural Mandate as a complement to, and expression of, the Great Commission.

But a funny thing happened on the way to the Capitol. If Wallis, Sider, and Mouw were trying to pull evangelicals back from their isolation out on the pietist end of the pendulum's arc, they didn't likely anticipate the degree to which the pendulum would swing the other way. (More work needs to be done to consider whether, Frankenstein-like, these moder-ate voices unwittingly unleashed the monster that would become the Religious Right.) In fact, evangelicals became such zealous converts to the Cultural Mandate that it has pretty much trumped the Great Com-mission. Christian leaders spend more time worrying about activist judges, Venezuelan dictators, and constitutional amendments than their evangelical forebears could ever have imagined. Devoting themselves to political strategizing and marshaling the machinations of government, evangelicals have so embraced participation in the "earthly city" that one wonders whether they've lost their passport to the City of God. Worse yet is the suspicion that evangelicals in America have just collapsed the two, such that the City of God is just downright confused with America as a city set on a hill.

And so we have Boyd's book.

Boyd's intervention into the discussion regarding evangelicals and politics is welcome. He is bold (1,000 members of his congregation left after hearing the sermons that gave birth to the book), passionate, and discerning, while trying to be as charitable as possible. He doesn't pull any punches, denouncing the nationalistic "idolatry" of American evangelical-ism which fuses the kingdom of God with a preferred, made-in-America version of the kingdom of the world, confusing and conflating the cross and the flag. Boyd unapologetically calls for a renewed Christian commitment to nonviolence, generously citing the Anabaptist refrains of John Howard Yoder, Stanley Hauerwas, and Lee Camp. (Both Rich Mouw's and Stanley Hauerwas's worst dreams have come true: Hauerwas has fallen into the hands of the pietists!)

But Boyd's claims can't be dismissed as the rantings of some Christian "leftist"; rather, one senses that these are the expressions of a pastor's broken heart, which every once in a while bubbles over into a kind of restrained, low-boil anger.

There is much to appreciate in Boyd's naming of the idolatries of the Religious Right. But the question is: does Boyd just get us swinging back to the other extreme of the pendulum? While I think he imagines himself as charting a third way, there are at least three factors of his alternative proposal that indicate this is simply a return to pietism:

1. Boyd operates with a number of distinctions which feel like good old dualisms. In particular, he paints a stark contrast between "the kingdom of the sword" and the "kingdom of the cross," or between "the kingdom of the world" and "the kingdom of God." While the distinction is important (it's exactly what is forgotten on the Constantinian end of the spectrum), Boyd's framing of it as an absolute dichotomy lacks a certain imagination. In particular, Boyd can't seem to imagine a good earthly kingdom — which seems to indicate the lack of both a robust creational theology and a lively eschatological imagination. After all, doesn't the heavenly city eventually make its way down to earth?

Because of this dichotomy, Boyd has to conclude that "no version of the kingdom of the world is closer to the kingdom of God than others." So this stark distinction entails a strange sort of relativism and precludes any ability to judge, in an *ad hoc* way, that one configuration of society looks more like the kingdom of God than any other. But can't we imagine the embodiment of the kingdom and so see in-breakings of the coming kingdom in the here-and-now, better in some places than others? For instance, I would guess that the kingdom looks more like a society that doesn't let illness and disease bankrupt a family than a society that distributes health "care" on the basis of market-driven principles.

2. This stark dichotomy has another consequence: the reemergence of "politics" as a realm basically untouched by the gospel. While he draws heavily on Anabaptists, Boyd seems more Lutheran on this point, sketching a kind of two-kingdom picture that relegates politics to the realm of an apathetic "whatever" — or more specifically, "however." In a number of places, Boyd remarks that "however" we decide to think about legal and ethical issues, what really matters is "our heart and motives."

He unpacks this by a curious exegesis of Jesus' calling of Matthew the tax collector and Simon the Zealot. Arguing from silence (a common ploy for Boyd), and noting the lack of any political commentary from Jesus about either of their political leanings, Boyd concludes that "Jesus invited them both to follow him *as they were,* prior to their transformation." Really? Or was he calling *both* of them to an entirely different, but common, politics?

This "however" relegation of politics to a matter of indifference means that, ultimately, Christ's call to discipleship doesn't touch our politics. In Boyd's stark rendition of the two kingdoms, the constant refrain is to simply "vote your conscience." This points to a persistent individualism that dominates his account. While he is eloquent about what the church can do to embody an alternative way of sacrificial, "power-under" love *for* the world, in the realm of politics you're on your own ("Vote your conscience!").

3. I'm suggesting that Boyd's prescription for evangelicals is a return to pietism because of the dualism and individualism of his constructive proposal. A third element also signals a return to pietism: a rather naïve distinction between what he sees as government's ability to merely "control behavior" in contrast to the church's ability to "transform hearts." By the end of the book, this translates into a de-emphasis on the systemic conditions of injustice and a renewed emphasis on "conversion" as a solution to social ills. "The goal of kingdom people," Boyd concludes, "must be to free the oppressor from his or her oppressed heart, which in turn frees those who are oppressed by them." For as he confidently claims, in a Dickensian spirit, "when hearts are transformed, behavior follows." One can almost see Scrooge making his way to the altar now.

It's hard to resist echoing Marx's point that transforming the hearts of capitalists wouldn't do a single thing to disturb the *systems* that fostered oppression of the proletariat. Indeed, unless he's out to judge the salvation of others (which he won't, given his antipathy toward "judgment" of any sort), wouldn't Boyd have to concede that there are all kinds of evangelicals in America with "transformed hearts" who quite readily pledge allegiance to the kingdom of the sword? Why do so many "born again" Christians look like everything Boyd is against?

Ultimately, I think this reflects Boyd's persistent dualism: politics and government work on the "outside," but the Holy Spirit works on the "inside." Government can control people's behavior, but the kingdom of God transforms hearts. But I think Boyd is wrong on both counts.

On the one hand, the practices associated with nationalistic rituals of the state don't just touch my "outside." To think this would be to fall into the erroneous assumption of Winston Smith in Orwell's *1984,* who mistakenly thought that, whatever Big Brother did to his body, they could never get to his inside — to his mind, his heart, his passions. But, of course, they did. Indeed, the chilling lesson of *1984* is that the machinations of the state could actually control what we *love.* Winston, you'll remember, ends up in love — with Big Brother.

On the other hand, the Spirit's transformation of hearts is not the kind of magic that Boyd suggests. Rather, the Spirit works through material, embodied practices of sanctification and discipleship aimed at forming citizens of the kingdom of God. Without those practices that "control behavior," the indwelling and transformative power of the Spirit will lie dormant and untapped.

So the question is: Is Boyd just inviting us back to more pietism? I'm worried that's the case. So perhaps the real question is: Can evangelical thinking about politics and cultural engagement escape the dialectical strictures of this either/or? Is there an alternative to "Constantinian" triumphalism (of either the left or right varieties) and "pietist" retreat? If evangelical political thought is going to escape this oscillation between unbiblical extremes, we must nurture a more nuanced and creative imagination.

Chapter 19
THE GOD OF AMERICANISM:
ON MITT ROMNEY'S "FAITH IN AMERICA"

BELIEFNET.COM'S "GOD-O-METER" HAS been sputtering and wheezing under the volume of God-talk on the presidential trail this past week. Mitt Romney's widely discussed speech on Thursday was followed by Obama/Oprah rallies that were peppered with religious references and articulated in the cadences of black preaching reminiscent of Martin Luther King Jr. Both were examples of "Faith in America."

But a lot can hang on a preposition. Romney first promised a speech about his faith, then backed off to offer a broader take on America's religious landscape and its heritage of religious freedom. So rather than offering an apologetic for his own faith, Romney instead offered an account of "Faith in America." But the speech has me wondering whether there's a difference; more specifically, I wonder what's at stake in that "in." From where I sit, it looks like Romney's "own" faith *is* faith *in America.* Americans needn't worry about Romney's Mormonism because, at the end of the day, the faith that trumps all others is "Americanism."

Don't get me wrong: this religion has a long and illustrious history (documented in David Gelertner's recent book, *Americanism: The Fourth Great Western Religion*). It is a noble faith that feeds off the blood of its martyrs — in particular "the greatest generation" to which Romney first appeals — who made the greatest sacrifice for the sake of the religion's

An earlier version of this essay appeared on the PBS Religion and Ethics Newsweekly "One Nation" blog at http://www.pbs.org/wnet/religionandethics/blog/2007/12/james-ka-smith-the-god-of-amer.html. Reprinted with permission.

highest value: *freedom* (understood, I should note, in largely negative terms as freedom of choice). Indeed, "freedom" and "liberty" are the mantras of this faith, and Romney's speech invokes these shibboleths no less than thirty times (God or "the Creator" or "divine author" comes in at a close second with twenty-one references). And Romney doesn't fail to allude to the great artifacts of this religion. Americanism has its own sacred documents (the Declaration of Independence and the Constitution) and its own saints ("the Founding Fathers"), and has even birthed its own cathedrals and grottos (just stroll the National Mall).

So if Mitt Romney was looking to quell concerns about his religion, I think he's performed admirably! He has indicated, in no uncertain terms, that he is an "Americanist" like almost every other presidential candidate (from I don't care *which* side of the aisle). He is an American before he is a Mormon. He is primarily interested in conserving America's role as a hegemon ("preserving American leadership" is the guise under which he segues to talk about religion). And he enthusiastically adopts Sam Adams's axiom that it's not the specifics of piety that matter, but rather whether one is a "patriot."

If conservatives were worried about his Mormonism, I think Romney has laid his cards on the table and said to them: "Look, don't worry. Mormonism doesn't prevent me from being an Americanist. We're brothers in that cause."

In a way, this is refreshingly honest theology. In fact, if one pays close attention to the actual theology at work here — that is, if one starts asking just *which* God is being invoked — one finds that it is a particular deity: "the divine 'author of liberty.'" The god of the culture warriors has always been a generic god of theism (precisely like the god of the Founding Fathers): a "God who gave us liberty" (to do what we want). The "Creator" is a granter of inalienable rights and unregulated freedoms, a god who shares and ordains "American values." Indeed, folks like Mark Lilla should find their hearts strangely warmed to find that Romney and other Americanists on the campaign trail happily praise the moralist gods of Rousseau and Kant. If evangelical culture warriors had worries about Romney's faith, his jeremiad today should confirm that he pledges allegiance to the same "God of liberty" that they do. We're all Americanists now.

Which is precisely why the Religious Right doesn't have the corner on this cult. American faith in libertarian freedom is so woven into the warp and woof of our political imagination that it is almost impossible for a presidential candidate to be agnostic with respect to the god of Americanism. The so-called Religious Left just focuses on different versions of negative freedom. Romney's Americanist god gives us the liberty of the market; Hillary Clinton's Americanist god gives me freedom to choose what I like when it comes to "my" body.

But I hope Mr. Romney and his culture warrior friends (whether on the right or left) won't be surprised if some of us find it hard to believe in Americanism and its god of liberty. Some of us just can't muster faith in the generic theism that is preached on the campaign trail, whether from the right or left. Some of us Christians have a hard time reconciling the Almighty, all-powerful, law-giving god of liberty with the crucified suffering servant born in a barn and executed at the hands of the elite. Some of us are trying to figure out what it means to be a people who follow one who relinquished his rights rather than asserted them, who considered submission a higher value than freedom. We serve a God-man who wasn't concerned with "preserving leadership" and the hegemony of the empire's gospel of freedom, but rather was crushed by its machinations for proclaiming and embodying another gospel.

We're not out to win a culture war; we're just trying to be witnesses. We're not out to "transform" culture by marshaling the engine of the state; we're trying to carve out little foretastes of a coming kingdom. And so we can't share the evangelistic zeal for the god of Americanism that is the orthodoxy of American presidential politics.

Chapter 20
CONSTANTINIANISM OF THE LEFT?
ON JIM WALLIS AND BARACK OBAMA

J IM WALLIS'S BOOK tour for *God's Politics* made a stop at Calvin
College last night. His presentation was disappointing (a lot of
slogan-mongering), but it was really his position that was disappointing — though not surprising, I must say. I'm glad to have gone, if only to
confirm my suspicions. There are a couple of areas in which Wallis either
gets it wrong or doesn't get it.

I would describe Wallis's position as a kind of Constantinianism of
the left. While he's not out to establish a theocracy governed by a leftish
god, his position is nevertheless deeply "statist." In terms articulated
by Daniel Bell in his important book *Liberation Theology After the End
of History,* Wallis still believes in "statecraft." What was most telling, I
thought, was that for all his talk about faith, and even "evangelicalism,"
last night, I don't know that he ever once mentioned the church. Instead,
he'll focus on "people of faith" getting out the vote, lobbying Congress,
and doing everything they can to marshal the political process to effect
prophetic justice. But that kind of picture plays right into the hands of
not only American liberal individualism but also the deep anti-ecclesial
individualism of evangelicalism. In contrast, I think the only hope for
justice is a robust church, which requires an ecclesiological account of
the formation of disciples. Wallis seems to think a good "moral" civics

This piece, and the following interview, first appeared on my public commentary blog,
Fors Clavigera.

lesson is enough. Indeed, at the end of the day, he thinks that democracy trumps the church, for as he put it (yes, this is a direct quote): "Religion must be disciplined by democracy."

I couldn't help but conclude that, whatever Wallis's earlier stance might have been, he's really just ended up as a humanist. The talk last night was riddled with talk of "values" — which is just the code word for some kind of vague, supposedly common American moral vision. So there's all kind of bluster about morals, faith, religion, and "values," but this is all aimed at the end of just creating a kinder, more compassionate American civil theology.

Now, given this critique of the Religious Left, let me state for the record (again!) that I am no fan, supporter, or sympathizer of the Religious Right. To the contrary. But there seems to be no shortage of Christian scholars, pundits, and armchair cultural critics pointing out the inadequacies, inconsistencies, and injustices of the Religious Right. Why repeat it here? Instead, I tend to be more motivated to point out the deficiencies of what passes for the "Religious Left" in this country. ("Left" is clearly a relative term, since I rarely hear the Christian "left" in this country really challenge the mechanisms of capitalist, market economies. Here a Victorian, Christian socialist like F. D. Maurice makes Jim Wallis sound like a PR rep for Wal-Mart. But I digress. . . .) Unfortunately, however, in the bifurcated world we inhabit, if you're not with us, you're against us. So my critique of the Christian Left is too often immediately mistaken as an indicator that I'm a card-carrying member of the Religious Right, or my critique of the Religious Right is (mis)taken as evidence that I'm part of that motley crew which is the Religious Left. Neither is the case.

Granted, Jim Wallis has tended to bear the brunt of my frustrations with the Christian Left — that stems, I suppose, from his visibility, and perhaps even from a kind of attitudinal proximity. Perhaps because I share so many of his concerns and criticisms (let that be noted for the record), it becomes even more important to highlight the differences — because I think a lot is at stake in the differences. But instead of focusing solely on Wallis, let me briefly consider Barack Obama's message of hope and change. I've been intrigued by the attention garnered by Senator Obama's address to a recent "Call to Renewal" Conference (a Jim Wallis outfit that does a lot of good work).

What's most disheartening in this is the way that Democrats still consider "religion" *instrumentally;* that is, they instrumentalize religion insofar as they see it as a strategy for accomplishing a goal. Look at the speech and consider closely just *how* "religion" is invoked by Obama:

> Now, such strategies of avoidance may *work* for progressives when our opponent is Alan Keyes. But over the long haul, I think we make a mistake when we fail to acknowledge the power of faith in people's lives — in the lives of the American people — and I think it's time that we join a serious debate about how to reconcile faith with our modern, pluralistic democracy. (Emphasis added)

The concern is with what will "work." And religion is seen as a way of connecting with the electorate, not as the *basis* for justice. Progressives need to "get religion," according to Obama, so that Democrats can communicate with religious people. But that is a *rhetorical,* not a religious point. This is confirmed later in Obama's speech when he says:

> And that is why, if we truly hope to speak to people where they're at — to communicate our hopes and values in a way that's relevant to their own — then as progressives, we cannot abandon the field of religious discourse.

Even when he later suggests this is "not just rhetorical," the direction of the point is still about how religious discourse will be "effective." (I do agree with Obama's point regarding the false requirements of "secularity.")

One even sees this instrumentalization of religion in Obama's testimony. He testifies that he was "drawn to the church," to be "in" the church, because of "the power of the African-American religious tradition to spur social change." Now, I certainly believe that justice is an essential aspect of the gospel, and I believe that being a disciple entails doing justice. But the temptation of the fundamentalism of the left is to make justice an end in itself. It might seem scandalous, but the gospel is not *only* — maybe not even primarily — about securing social justice. This is why worship and liturgy and Eucharist play such marginal roles in what the Christian

Left has to say about "church" — the Left Church is an organization of activists, not a community of worshipers. This is also why the left is more comfortable talking about "faith" than about "the church." But even if the goal is a good one (like eradicating poverty), if Christian faith is seen as an instrument to another end, then faith is *de facto* penultimate. And that, I would suggest, is precisely the formula of idolatry — and, in fact, a mirror of the way religion is "used" by the Religious Right (just for different "ends").

Thus it's not surprising when Obama finally sells the farm, claiming (like Jim Wallis) that religion must be disciplined by the demands of democracy. Obama puts it this way:

> Democracy demands that the religiously motivated translate their concerns into universal, rather than religion-specific, values. It requires that their proposals be subject to argument, and amenable to reason. I may be opposed to abortion for religious reasons, but if I seek to pass a law banning the practice, I cannot simply point to the teachings of my church or evoke God's will. I have to explain why abortion violates some principle that is accessible to people of all faiths, including those with no faith at all.

I recognize the unique constraints of inhabiting a pluralist state. But Obama opens himself up to a disturbing logic here (and treads on questions of faith and reason that are out of his league, I think). With this formulation, Obama creates a kind of "two truths" framework: I can know or be convinced that something is true in (at least) two ways: (1) based on "religious reasons," stemming from revelation, and (2) based on "universal" principles of (just plain) "reason." While I reject the existence of the latter, I'll set that aside here. Let's take Obama's framework: what this means is that while I might believe and know something to be wrong on the basis of "religious reasons," unless I can find a "universal" reason to make the case for that in the "public" sphere, then I cannot expect to legislate the point. I can't expect something to become policy by appealing only to religious reasons.

I agree with the opposition to theocracy, and I agree that distinctly religious positions should not be legislated by the state. But what Obama can't seem to imagine is that one might, in fact, pass on the state in order to hold the integrity of what one "knows" on the basis of "religious reasons." I just can't imagine the kind of bifurcated identity that Obama's framework requires — a fractured identity in which, when there is conflict, it is the requirements of "universal" reason which must trump what one knows on the basis of religious faith. From what I can gather, Obama is pro-choice precisely because he doesn't think he can come up with a "universal," rational argument against abortion. (I think it's also because, like almost everyone — Democrat and Republican — he's a libertarian at heart.) And so, *as a politician,* he is pro-choice. If he's going to play by the rules of the pluralist state, and stay within the bounds of the Constitution, he has to set aside his religious beliefs.

But what about another possibility? What about setting aside participation in a state and politics which require such bifurcation? What about opting out of a democratic rationality which demands ultimate allegiance? Instead of Wallis's and Obama's leftish civil theology, I'll continue to believe that our most important political action remains the act of discipleship through worship.

Chapter 21

LEFTISH CONSTANTINIANISM
REVISITED: AN INTERVIEW

AFTER SEVERAL POSTS on my blog, *Fors Clavigera,* articulated a critique of Jim Wallis and the Religious Left (now comprising material in chapter 20 above), a couple of avid bloggers — Eric Austin Lee and Dale Lature — conducted a blog interview with me on some of the issues. Their helpful questions get at some important issues, so I thought readers might find it helpful if I reproduce the "interview" here.

LEE AND LATURE: Thank you for being open to this discussion with Dale and me. Yesterday, we crafted a few questions that we thought would help clarify your critique of Jim Wallis of Sojourners. All three of us have seen or met Jim Wallis in person on his latest book tour, and Dale has been following Wallis and the work of Sojourners for the last twenty years. The questions below are in response to your blog post on *Fors Clavigera* called "Constantinianism on the Left?"

Pertaining to language, how does one speak truth to power without "ceding too much to the state" in such a way that one avoids being "statist" and yet still speaks to the state, in what one might call "accessible" language, so that the state can best be "called to task"? Is this even possible, or are we called to speak differently?

JAMES K. A. SMITH: This way of putting the question still assumes a certain confidence and hope in the state, which I think is misplaced. I don't think it's a matter of calling the state "to task." I think it's more a matter of showing the state what it can never be: a properly ordered community lovingly aimed at bearing the image of the Triune God. The notion of speaking "to" the state with the hope that the state will "get" it works from a misplaced confidence that this is even possible. I don't deny that, on good liberal, capitalist grounds, one could perhaps convince "the state" to stop killing children in Iraq or Taiwan, but to consider that a "success" would be to adopt quite a utilitarian criteria.

This question seems to work from a picture of the church (or "Christians," as I think Wallis would put it — or maybe even just "people of faith") talking "to" the state with the hope of getting the state to agree with her/them. I'm just not sure that such a dialogue is either possible or desirable. In my more cynical moments, I think it's casting pearls before swine. The church is not called to engage in some kind of apologetic project to "convince" the state to do "the right thing" (which the state, per se, could never properly recognize). Rather, the church is called to model the kingdom for the world, showing the world what it cannot be apart from the regenerating power of the Spirit. The church should model the in-breaking of the kingdom to the state, but not with the misguided hopes that the state could enact this in federal policy.

L&L: How is it that Wallis ends up "humanist"? We understand your perception of the telos of Wallis's language (with which Dale is in disagreement), but into what particular definition of a "humanist" does this tie?

JKAS: Grant that there was meant to be a certain rhetorical flourish in this description of Wallis as a "humanist." But what I meant by this was that Wallis, by trying to generically appeal to "values" (gag!) or "people of faith," was reducing the particularity of the church's theological articulation of "the good" and thinking that this can be translated into a generally available and accessible notion of "justice" — unhooked from the real particularities of Christian confession. This is why I describe his project as a "Constantinianism of the left." Wallis is working with a covert natural theology: he thinks that the "core values" of biblical justice can be articulated, legitimated, and adopted apart from the particularities of scriptural revelation and narrative. He thinks he can show that "biblical" justice just makes "good sense" to Congressional representatives and voters. But this mitigates the scandal of particularity. I would prefer Milbank's formulation: "Can morality be Christian?" His answer is a resounding "No."

By the way, I think Eugene McCarraher's recent article in *Books and Culture* ("The Revolution Begins in the Pews," May/June 2005) articulates a similar critique of Wallis's *God's Politics,* especially when he suggests that the book is an "exemplary artifact of religious liberalism, the leftish and weaker variant of the civil religion" (p. 27). Those who lack imagination will think that this is a "conservative" judgment; it's not.

Chapter 22
THE LAST PROPHET OF LEVIATHAN:
ON MARK LILLA'S *THE STILLBORN GOD*

I T WOULD BE unfortunate if Lilla's *The Stillborn God* got lost in the shuffle of the burgeoning industry of Theocracy Alarmists, Inc. (fronted by the likes of Chris Hedges, Kevin Phillips, and Randall Balmer) — or even worse, lumped in with the screeds of secular fundamentalists like Christopher Hitchens and Sam Harris. Unlike these other slapdash offerings to fawning secularist audiences, Lilla's book is winsome, erudite, and engaging. Even critics will have to recognize that this is a stunning book.

It is also a handsome book, just the sort of thing one expects from Knopf: stout and meaty in a 5×8 format with a textured dust-jacket and creamy pages — a pleasure to hold and (I have to confess) caress. Only deckled pages would have been an improvement. Such lovely materiality deserves praise.

But back to the first claim: What makes the book stunning is the fact that Lilla, if you'll forgive the semiotic jargon, is a helluva storyteller. Let's not underestimate his achievement. *The Stillborn God* is so lucid that it lulls you into thinking you actually understand Kant and Hegel. Giants in German theology like Schleiermacher and Troeltsch are adroitly encapsulated in a few pages, and relatively minor figures like Gogarten or Cohen stride onto the stage as such vibrant characters in the story that one is compelled by their amplified presence. Lilla uniquely weds the analytic

"The Last Prophet of Leviathan," *Perspectives,* April 2008, pp. 20-22. Reprinted with permission.

skill of an expositor with the storytelling skills of a dramatist. This is as close as Hegel is ever going to get to "creative non-fiction."

Lilla's erudition informs a sweeping narrative from late medieval Christendom up to the outbreak of World War II. But it is a tale with a curious narrative arc: the hero emerges early, but the remainder of the story tracks all the ways he is forgotten by later *dramatis personae* — such that only the narrator (Lilla) seems to honor his memory. The story goes something like this:

We begin with a crisis, the so-called "wars of religion": awash in the fervor and passion of religious faith, the early modern West finds itself spiraling into the chaotic violence of religious wars which are the result of a toxic mix of theology and politics that Lilla simply describes as "political theology." Into this milieu of religio-political violence strides our hero, Thomas Hobbes, engineer of the "Great Separation" that sequestered theology (with its claims to divine revelation) from having any role or authority in matters of "politics" (which was to be conducted on the basis of public reason available to and agreed upon by all). Thus was "modern political philosophy" born as the antidote to "political theology." Hobbes and political philosophy liberated "us" *(sic)* from the "Kingdom of Darkness" (a phrase that gets repeated just often enough that it takes on a kind of Michael Moore–ish quality, I'm afraid).

To this point, up to Locke's liberalization of Hobbes, Lilla's story is not especially unique. It's a classic example of what Charles Taylor would call a "subtraction" story of modernity. But things get interesting when Lilla continues to consider the fate of this Great Separation after Hobbes. From this point the story becomes a jeremiad, lamenting the ways in which Hobbes's heirs (Rousseau, Kant, Hegel) rolled back the accomplishments of the father of "modern political philosophy," giving just enough ground to religion and theology that political theology would once again rear its ugly head right here in the "enlightened" West. Rousseau and Kant both re-admit (an albeit scaled-down, "rational") religion back into public political discussion. Something about human nature and human morality pressed them to give a continuing though chastened role to religion for even "modern" man. But keeping the door open just a tiny bit was fateful: what began as a toe in the door ends up as the elephant in the room. Thus Lilla plays Samuel to Rousseau and Kant's Saul: "What's this bleating of sheep I hear?" Why have you not vanquished every vestige of political theology? Making room for even a "modern" political theology as purveyed by the liberal theology of Schleiermacher or Cohen gives rise to a Frankenstein-ish monster that comes back to haunt "the West" in the form of "German Christianity" (indeed, the book might have been better subtitled *Religion, Politics, and Modern Germany*).

Admittedly, one of the places where Lilla's storytelling goes off the rails is his account of twentieth-century German theology, and of Barth in particular, upon whom he lays the blame for Nazism. Only someone as deft as Lilla could make such a claim seem even remotely plausible, but at the end of the day it remains a ludicrous charge. But I'll leave it to the Princeton police to protect Barth.

The lesson Lilla draws from this morality tale is that the "God" that would have issued from the Great Liberal Separation was a "stillborn God" — a superfluous deity easily lopped off by Occam's razor. After all, just what work does such a god do? What does such a non-interventionist, deistic, distant bestower of human autonomy add to the universe? Why bother? "To the decisive questions — 'Why be a Christian?' 'Why be a Jew?' — liberal theology offered no answer at all" (pp. 301-2). Most people need more than that.

But not "us." It is perhaps the pronouns that are most telling in *The Stillborn God.* Throughout the book I found myself wondering: Just who is this for? What's the point? Why is this story important? For whom? This is hinted at in the opening but clarified in a final coda: the story is intended as a cautionary tale for "us." "The rebirth of political theology is a humbling story," Lilla concludes, "or ought to be" (p. 302) for those of us with the intellectual will and fortitude to choose to be "heirs to the Great Separation" (p. 306).

At this point Lilla turns aside to the small cadre of the Enlightened who see the story for what it is: "Those of us who have accepted the heritage of the Great Separation must do so soberly. Time and again we must remind ourselves that we are living an experiment, that *we* are the exceptions" (p. 308). Wavering between insider code and an invitation to join this inner circle of the exceptional, Lilla ends with a manifesto of inverse gnosticism:

"We have chosen to keep our politics unilluminated by the light of revelation. If our experiment is to work, we must rely on our own lucidity" (p. 309). "We" turns out to be the sect of modern-day Essenes living on the upper West Side, who have vowed to abstain from the illusions of the masses and have consigned themselves to the cold, hard desert "reality" disclosed by reason. Lilla and his exceptionalist monastic brotherhood of enlightened "us" have girded their loins in order to make their way in the world without the comforts of faith and revelation (I'm guessing one would bump into Hitchens and Harris in the same rationalist desert after all).

Where does that leave the rest of us — the us not included in Lilla's enlightened "us"? I, for one, am not persuaded to drop my nets and follow Hobbes.

A first core problem of the book is the very beginning of the story: it buys into the simplistic myth of religious violence and secular peace, resting on the unsubstantiated empirical claim that "religion" (whatever that is) breeds violence whereas institutions of liberal democracy foster peace (current world conflicts in the name of "democracy" notwithstanding). Thus Lilla repeats the liberal alarm about religion's "passion" and "fervor" as the incubator of violence — passions to be curbed by the machinations of Leviathan and, later, the liberal democratic state. But this is a distinction that is untenable for anyone who has ever attended a professional sports event in the United States. It sounds as if Lilla has never witnessed the fervor and passion incited at the opening of a NASCAR race when the dancing colors of the flag are mingled with the iconography of a military fly-over. The opening prayer certainly doesn't excite the same passions!

In short, the myth of distinctly religious violence and liberal peace is untenable. As the work of William Cavanaugh has demonstrated, the so-called "wars of religion" were primarily about statecraft, and "religion" was an invention of the *politiques* behind the modern state. While we might not expect Lilla to be a theologian, he is culpably responsible for his ignorance of Cavanaugh's trenchant challenge to the tired liberal story about the "wars of religion." If that story is placed in doubt, then the liberal state is not the savior it pretends to be. Leviathan is more perpetrator than liberator. And Lilla can't simply plead that he's "doing history"; what's at stake is his *historiography*.

A second core problem is a related distinction between "political theology" and "modern political philosophy." While he never quite clarifies the nature of the distinction, political theology is seen to be problematic because it appeals to revelation, whereas political philosophy subscribes to a kind of epistemological asceticism that resigns itself to the "human all too human." Modern political philosophy is thus more "realistic," according to Lilla, and in this sense has a leg up on the illusions or dishonesty of political theology.

But this, too, is an untenable distinction. This is not a tension between faith and reason, theology and the secular. It is always already a tension between two faiths, between *competing* theologies, between rival *stories* about the world — neither of which can be "proved" but both of which are affirmed by faith. While I think Lilla has conveniently (and irresponsibly) ignored scholarship along these lines (as articulated in the work of John Milbank, Nicholas Wolterstorff, and Jeffrey Stout), in fact his own account admits the point. As he observes, Hobbes is not without faith: "On the very first page of his work Hobbes makes an implicit profession of faith: that to understand religion and politics, we need not understand anything about God; we need only understand man as we find him, a body alone in the world" (p. 76). Not all theologies require appeal to revelation; theologies bubble up from the fundamental, faith-based stories we tell about the world. In this respect, modern political philosophy is always already a political theology. Leviathan is not without its priests and prophets. Lilla's story about liberation *from* theology is informed by an *alternative* theology. That fact calls into question his entire project.

Picturing Faith: Criticism

Chapter 23
ABSENCE AS A WINDOW:
ON THE POETRY OF FRANZ WRIGHT

MANY IMAGINE WRITING poetry as therapy — a way to exorcise demons. But the result is often indulgent sentimentalism. In place of a Germanic notion of the poet as conduit of the gods, we get the poet as the chronicler of her symptoms, reveling in disclosures that are at once embarrassing, narcissistic, and immune to criticism (who are *you* to question *my* feelings?). One can see this therapeutic reductionism embodied in the television series *Rescue Me,* where firefighter Kenny Shea emotes terrible poetry as a mode of post–9/11 healing. This portrait of the artist as therapeut inundates us with revelations of secrets and sins, unleashing demon after demon in a confessional deluge that leaves us protesting: too much information! (I say all this despite my admiration for Anne Sexton, whose work is particularly susceptible to this kind of criticism.)

If any poet could use therapy, it's Franz Wright. And in fact, he has received it. Abandoned by his Pulitzer Prize–winning father, the poet James Wright, Franz the son spiraled into a life of addiction and mental illness, spending time on the precipice during two years in a mental health hospital in the mid-1990s. But Wright's poetry isn't his therapy; rather, it is a witness to exorcism by other means.

Indeed, one of the most interesting aspects of Wright's intensely

"Absence as a Window [on *God's Silence* by Franz Wright]," *Harvard Divinity Bulletin* 35.1 (Winter 2007): 83-86. Reprinted with permission.

spiritual poetry is the absence of self-helpism that attends the poetry-as-therapy school. For at root, the poetry-as-therapy line remains confident in the powers of the poet to pull himself up by his bootstraps. "Poet, save thyself!" comes the challenge. "Don't mind if I do," the poet/therapist replies. In contrast, Wright's poetry is a testimony to the helplessness of the poet — of anyone — in the face of the horrors that attend our broken lives. What's needed is an in-breaking of *grace;* poetry then comes along trying to find words to name the event of that in-breaking from elsewhere. But if the poet can find the words, then the poem becomes an invitation to others to be hopeful and open to such grace. In contrast, the narcissism of self-helpism often leaves the broken-hearted even more despairing, since they can't imagine mustering that kind of voice and chutzpah to take on the demons themselves.

Wright has commented that part of his recovery, which included his conversion to Catholicism, involved letting go of poetry as a substitute theology. "For me," he said, "poetry was a kind of religion in and of itself for a long time. I believed in poetry. I had an almost theological conception of it. But I came to realize that was a mistake." What makes Wright's poetry so spiritually inviting, and even theologically suggestive, stems from this sense of poetry's being positioned by grace.

REDEEMING ABSENCE

Since emerging from those darkest days, Wright's star has steadily ascended. His 2000 collection, *The Beforelife,* was nominated for the Pulitzer, and his subsequent offering, *Walking to Martha's Vineyard* (2003), won the prize. His latest collection, *God's Silence* (2006), completes what could be read as a trilogy with a kind of narrative arc. Not a tale of progress or even progressive sanctification, but more like the landscape of Book 10 of Augustine's *Confessions,* where even the bishop has bad days.

I was first drawn to Wright's poetry in one of those wonderful sites of God's providence: the clearance bin at a Book Mart in Los Angeles. Happening upon *The Beforelife,* I was hooked by the absence that resonated through the book — the absence of a father in particular. Having been estranged from my own father for twenty years, and having not even set eyes on him for at least a dozen years at the time, I found that Wright's laments named the absence in my own life, most powerfully in "Goodbye":

> *But I have overcome you*
> *in myself,*
> *I won't behave*
>
> *like you,*
> *so you*
>
> *can't hurt me now;*
>
> *so you are not*
> *going*
>
> *to hurt me again*
>
> *and I, I can't*
> *happen*
> *to you.*

The 2000 and 2003 collections are haunted by a "You" — a second-person interlocutor of some ambiguity, and one isn't always sure which father/Father is under consideration here ("At ten/I turned you into a religion," the poet remarks) culminating in "Flight," a heart-wrenching poem of the father and son meeting, but certainly not communing. In this poem, included in *Walking to Martha's Vineyard,* the absence of his father takes on an omnipresence that echoes the psalter:

> *If I'm walking the streets of a city*
> *covering every square inch of the continent*
> *all its lights out*
> *and empty of people,*
> *even then you are there*

The absence has the presence of a scar, making him a marked man: "Since you left me at eight I have always been lonely/star-far from the person right next to me, but/closer to me than my bones you/you are there."

But if his wounds are craters of absence, there is yet a sense in which Wright's poetry redeems absence — as if the hole carved by his father's departure somehow also cut open a channel for grace. For emerging regularly and rhythmically with and in the absence is hope. "Flight," for instance, ends with a dream sequence of Franz talking and laughing with his father. But even as a general trope, one finds Wright, in Bono's words cribbed from Bruce Cockburn, kicking the darkness until it bleeds daylight. So in the same poem ("One Heart"), the poet recounts how "this morning a young woman/described what it's like shooting coke with a baby/in your arms," but then concludes with a doxology of gratitude:

> *Thank You for letting me live for a little as one of the*
> *sane; thank You for letting me know what this is*
> *like. Thank You for letting me look at your frightening*
> *blue sky without fear, and your terrible world without*
> *terror, and your loveless psychotic and hopelessly*
> *lost*
> *with this love*

The Catholic philosopher Jean-Luc Marion has suggested that the really revelatory site of the icon — its revelational sweet-spot, one might say — is the dark pupil of the eye that invites us through it like a window. One could say that Franz Wright sees absence in this iconic manner: as a window, a portal to transcendence. It is in God's hiding that he shows himself, and it's just this absence that staves off madness. Madness, after all, isn't the result of the world dissolving into nothingness before our eyes, but rather of the incessant deluge of reality that overwhelms us. Madness comes not from absence but from excess presence. And so for the one who feels pressed on every side by a world that is *too* present and keeps imposing itself without respite, absences are a gift. Thus Wright concludes "Cloudless Snowfall" with an off-handed note of gratitude: "and/by the way thank You for/keeping Your face hidden, I/can hardly bear the beauty of this world."

FAITH AND MADNESS

While Wright, Jacob-like, manages to wrestle a blessing from the dark spaces of absence, this is not to suggest that his poetry is triumphalist, dreamy, or utopian. To the contrary, especially in the earlier collections, the shards of hope are respites that let us briefly emerge onto the surface for air before being submerged again into the depths of depression. The meditations that emerge from his time in a mental institution are particularly haunting, arriving like scrawled messages in a bottle sent from some far-off island right there in east Boston. But one has the impression that if Franz Wright was standing right next to you at the time, he would have been far off. And so the poems from the period have an almost extra-terrestrial quality about them. Or at least an exotic even voyeuristic feel about them, such that the reader feels as if the poet is a patient (not yet a cadaver) cut open on the table for all to see. (Something like the guilty pleasure of Phillipe de Broca's film *Le roi de coeur (King of Hearts)* taking us through the gates and into the asylum.)

This is displayed in the opening piece of *God's Silence*, "East Boston, 1996," wherein Wright admits: "I knew I looked like a suicide/returning an overdue book to the library." The bus ride is an occasion for "some diverting speculations/on the comparative benefits/of waiting in front of a ditch to be shot/alone or in company/of others, and then whether one would prefer/these last hypothetical others/to be friends, family, enemies, total/or relative strangers. Would you hold hands?"

But what's interesting is the very tenuous fulcrum on which Wright's world turns. I imagine it as one of those flashy, hologram baseball cards. Hold it one way and Derek Jeter is squared up in the batter's box, ready for the pitcher's delivery. But turn the card just ever so slightly, and the whole picture changes, and Jeter has uncoiled and exploded, sending the ball hurtling to the left field wall. The picture only needs to pivot a slight bit and the whole scene changes.

A lot of saints and others seem to inhabit the world close to that fulcrum. On bad days the world is a dark, cold monstrosity; but on other days, on a good day, the picture tilts just a bit, and all of a sudden the world breaks open and shows us something we couldn't see before. Wright's poetry teeters on this fulcrum, too. "I just noticed," he'll write, "that it is my own private/National I Hate Myself and Want to Die Day/(which means the next day I will love my life/and want to live forever)."

There's a fine line, it's been said, between faith and madness; indeed, faith *as* madness has a long pedigree from Paul (1 Cor. 1–2) to Kierkegaard. (A picture of Wright in *Poets & Writers* shows Joakim Garff's mammoth biography of Kierkegaard on the floor beside his chair.) Wright's poetry attests that only a world that totters on the edge of nothingness could turn in such a way as to be revelatory and translucent.

SILENCE SPEAKS

The sense that absence is revelatory feeds into another theme that reaches its crescendo in *God's Silence:* the paradoxical principle that silence speaks. Just as God's hiding is not concealment but manifestation, so also, for Wright, God's silence is not that of one who refuses to speak, but rather whose silence speaks volumes. This is counterintuitive for many. For those of us who cut our teeth on Francis Schaeffer, we have been indelibly marked by the claim that *He Is There and He Is Not Silent,* and embedded in this is an imperative from humanity to God: "If you're there, *say* something!" But Wright's poetry struggles to make sense of a silence that speaks *more* than words — silence as a kind of "tongues" that exceeds words. And so the poet is confronted with a challenge not unlike the theologian or the preacher: How to put into words that which exceeds them, including the silences that say so much? What would it mean for poetry to testify to such silence?

In "From a Discarded Image" (in *Beforelife*), Wright struggles with this as a threat of violence, the harm that can be done to "the world's wordless beauty" by the words of the poet. Later, in "Icon from Childhood," Wright picks up an Augustinian line regarding words as things and all things as signs, but sees through them to their emptiness:

that these words
are only

things, *but*
that all things are shining
words, busy
silently
saying themselves —
they don't need me.

But in *God's Silence,* the theme begins to take on echoes of the psalter (indeed, the cadences and rhythms of Wright's poetry live off of the liturgy and the Scriptures). This is embedded in a refrain that appears six times in six different poems, first announcing itself in "The Hawk," where Wright reflects on "this three-pound lump/of sentient meat electrified/by hope and terror has learned to hear/His silence like the sun." That trope — "I heard God's silence like the sun" — returns as a chorus throughout the collection, and seems to allude to Psalm 19, where the psalmist points to a declaration that exceeds and transcends language. The words of Wright's poems are trying to be this kind of oblique pointer. This requires relinquishing the poetic pretension to "capturing" experience.

The long silences need to be loved, perhaps
more than the words
which arrive
to describe them
in time.

Franz Wright's poetry invites us to the edge: to that risky precipice where words succeed in their failure; to that frightening fulcrum where the world teeters, back and forth, between abyss and icon; and to the dark corners of a broken-hearted world where there are holes cut out for the grace to get in.

Chapter 24

DUMBING DOWN DISCERNMENT?

THE HEGEMONY OF THE POPULAR

ESCHEWING THE DUALISM that has plagued American fundamentalism, the Reformed tradition has emphasized that the work of culture-making — the human unfolding of creational potential — is not only a necessary task, but a *good* one. It has therefore sought to encourage not only cultural discernment and engagement, but also genuine cultural production. And one of the most important spheres of cultural engagement, discernment, and production has been in the realm of the arts. Here at Calvin this finds significant, and perhaps primary, expression through engagement with music and film.

But the Reformed tradition, as heir to the Protestant Reformation, has also been a *leveling* tradition. There is a marked anti-clericalism and anti-elitism in the Reformed tradition's DNA. Indeed, the Reformation spawned a sense that God was equally available to everyone and thus there were no privileged channels of access, no special "orders" of "religious" men and women; rather, God was as present and available to you and me as any priest or confessor.

Originally appeared as "Dumbing Down Discernment? Part 1: The Hegemony of the Popular," *Uncompressed* 1.3 (March 2007): 2-4, and "Dumbing Down Discernment? Part 2: The Tyranny of the Contemporary," *Uncompressed* 1.4 (April 2007). *Uncompressed* is a publication of the Student Activities Office at Calvin College. Reprinted with permission.

This leveling tendency or egalitarian streak has been translated into Reformed thinking about the arts: one of the common themes of Reformed "aesthetics" (philosophical reflection on the nature of art) has been a persistent interest in questioning the distinction between "high" culture and "low" culture. Or perhaps to put it otherwise, the tradition of Reformed aesthetics (as seen in the work of Cal Seerveld or Nicholas Wolterstorff) has persistently sought to revalue the artistic and creative expressions that bubble up in "popular" culture, valuing the handiwork of artisans and the lyrical expressions of minstrels and troubadours of every sort.

On the one hand, I think this is right on the money and an important aspect of Reformed thinking about culture in general, and the arts in particular. But I wonder if this line of thinking has run amok in our contemporary climate. In voices like Seerveld and Wolterstorff, the valuing of "low" culture (though they wouldn't be fans of that phrase) was never to the neglect of the expressions of "high" culture. If Seerveld and Wolterstorff invited us to take seriously the work of folk crafts and popular music, they certainly weren't encouraging us to ignore the artistic expressions of symphonies and opera. While this Reformed "leveling" made us attentive to the genius embedded in the music of Thom Yorke or the films of Wes Anderson, it was never meant to distract us from the symphonies of Rachmaninov or the rich, textured novels of Evelyn Waugh.

But I fear that, in our contemporary context, the Reformed valuing of "popular" culture has come at the expense of "high" culture. We can cite reams of *Seinfeld* dialogue, but not a line of Hopkins. As teachers, we pepper our lectures with U2 or Coldplay lyrics in hopes of hooking the imagination of our students, but invocations of dialogue from Oscar Wilde plays fall on deaf ears. We can discourse on "redemptive" themes in *The Simpsons* (for goodness sake!), but have no familiarity with the landscapes of transcendence in Graham Greene novels.

I fear that the leveling tendency of Reformed aesthetics has brought about a "dumbing down" of discernment and cultural engagement. And that, without question, is a loss. We've spent so much time valuing popular culture, it has come at the expense of the riches of "high" culture. We've devoted so much ink and energy to convincing students that God shows up in the frames of *American Beauty* or the lyrics of Johnny Cash that they've stopped looking for him in the genius of Bach's motets or the romance of Rossetti's poetry.

This hit home for me as I've been working on a new book called *Desiring the Kingdom*. The book will lay out a vision of the human person — and thus discipleship — governed by the dynamics of love and desire. Imagination is a central aspect of who we are as "desiring agents," and so I want to expound this by drawing on visions of the human person as expressed in the arts — especially imaginative construals of love. And here's where the poverty of popular culture's hegemony hits home. Whereas I want to draw on the wells of imaginative wisdom embedded in Waugh's *Brideshead Revisited* and Walker Percy's *Love in the Ruins,* those references won't land with a student readership which considers the Sundance Channel "highbrow." Because we've settled for the thinness of popular culture as the *lingua franca* of cultural capital, I'm stuck working with *Moulin Rouge* and the lyrics of Radiohead. Not that these aren't interesting, provocative sources; but they don't come close to offering the revelations found in those novels.

And so I fear that the Reformed emphasis on valuing popular culture has transmuted into a dumbing-down of discernment. What if we marshaled our energetic passion for culture and began to channel more of that towards an appreciation of "high" culture? What if we spent a little less time watching movies and a little more time reading poetry and literature? What if we traded some of our iPod space devoted to Sufjan and carved out some room for Vivaldi? Wouldn't *that* be counter-cultural and resist the sound-bite-ization of a commercialized culture? What if the church could be an agent of and invitation to "high" culture? Might it be the case that sometimes redemption is redemption *from* the hegemony of popular culture?

THE TYRANNY OF THE CONTEMPORARY

I'm suggesting that the shape of our cultural engagement has remained captive to a kind of dumbing-down that is a reflection of the broader commercial culture whose cultural diet has been reduced to the sound bite.

Thus the redemption of culture might involve revaluing "high" culture and resisting the lowest-common-denominator approach of popular culture. This doesn't mean there are not "everyday apocalypses" in Coldplay or *Children of Men*. I just don't think they have the intensity and depth of the revelational moments in the literature and music of "high" or "classical" culture.

Just as Christian cultural engagement should resist the hegemony of the popular, so too should we resist the tyranny of the contemporary. The drug of novelty is a powerful addiction in our culture. We regularly deride cultural phenomena for being "*so* five-minutes-ago!" A 24/7 news cycle has media outlets clamoring for "scoops" around the clock, issuing in a stream of "revelations" about the exploits of Paris Hilton. I experienced this most intensely while living in Los Angeles, one of our nation's most prolific cultural producers — but also the epicenter of the tyranny of the contemporary. "What have you done for me *lately?*" is the quintessential L.A. mantra (expressed so well in Christopher Guest's satire, *For Your Consideration*). Even the (hideous!) architecture of Los Angeles articulates this fixation on the present.

This finds expression closer to home as well. If the arts provide a *lingua franca* for conversation, I find that the tyranny of the contemporary has produced only a Babel of tribal references. Trying to invoke wisdom embedded in popular culture, my allusions to the Indigo Girls or Bruce Cockburn draw blank stares. My friend's second installment of a course on U2 found a less receptive audience since the band hadn't released an album within the past year. And while syndication and TBS stem the tide somewhat, even *Seinfeld* references are less and less of a hook.

This general privileging of the contemporary (which finds a correlate in the cultural idolization of youth — witness the Botox industry!) has at least two consequences: First, the tyranny of the contemporary fosters a terrible case of memory loss. The drug of novelty produces a contemporary snobbery that looks down its nose at the past and previous, cynically snickering at what has come before — but thereby shutting down any openness to the wisdom of the past. Second, this memory loss affects the bonds of community. As Quentin Schultze has remarked, the tyranny of the contemporary results in a contraction or compression of our sense of "generation."[1] My "generation" is the group of people who have consumed the same media in three-year cycles. On this account, seniors at Calvin think of freshmen as constituting another generation! Imagine the gap between freshmen and a decrepit old professor who's 36 years old! This translates into a disconnect not only in the context of the college, but also within our churches, such that churches carve themselves up into specific niches — "boutique" churches that cater to smaller and smaller generational segments of the ancient body of Christ.

There is a sense in which Christians are to be a people "untimely born," as Paul says of himself (1 Cor. 15:8). This is not because we are traditional*ists* who slavishly and nostalgically long for "the old ways" (Jer. 6:16). However, there is a deep sense in which the church is a people called to resist the "presentism" embedded in the tyranny of the contemporary. We are called to be a people of *memory,* who are shaped by a tradition that is millennia older than the last Billboard chart. And we are also called to be a people of *expectation,* praying for and looking forward to a coming Kingdom that will break in upon our present like a thief in the night. We are a *stretched* people, citizens of a kingdom that is both older and newer than anything offered by "the contemporary."

I think our cultural engagements and our cultural making should reflect this stretching. As cultural discerners who are "untimely born," we should have something of an "old soul" within us, making us attentive and attuned to riches of a cultural past — which are often more oriented to the future than the presentism of contemporary culture. The tyranny of the contemporary yields much art that suffers not only from memory loss but also from a paucity of expectation and *hope.* Instead we get cynicism. Christian cultural engagement and production should exhibit the attitude one critic has attributed to the nineteenth-century Pre-Raphaelites: "avant-garde archaism."

1. See Quentin Schultze, "He-Man and the Masters of the Universe: Media, Postmodernity and Christianity," in *Imagination and Interpretation: Christian Perspectives,* ed. Hans Boersma (Vancouver: Regent College Publishing, 2005), p. 156. I don't share Schultze's penchant for pinning all of this on "postmodernism," however; rather, I would say that this tyranny of the contemporary is a facet of *hyper*-modernism. For discussion, see James K. A. Smith, *Who's Afraid of Postmodernism?* (Grand Rapids: Baker Academic, 2006), ch. 5.

Perhaps I could suggest a link between the riches of "high" culture and a "classic" culture of the past: the intensity and depth of apocalypse in the riches of the cultural tradition leave a mark of grace that is deep, and one that endures over time. Like the initials of lovers carved deep into the trunk of an old tree, they stand the test of time and continue to speak; whereas too many contemporary cultural offerings are merely light etchings that will barely survive one winter of erosion.

So I have suggested that Christian cultural engagement should invite us up and back: "up" to the riches of "high" culture which are not easily digested by a dumbed-down public discourse, and "back" to the riches of the "classics" in painting, literature, music, and poetry.

Chapter 25

THE DEVIL READS DERRIDA: FASHION, FRENCH PHILOSOPHY, AND POSTMODERNISM

PHILOSOPHERS REGULARLY HAVE to make apologies for their profession. Very rare is the parent who erupts in joy when a daughter or son comes home at Thanksgiving announcing that they're going to major in philosophy. This inevitably sounds like preparation for any number of careers that involve various permutations of the question, "Would you like fries with that?" So how could philosophy have any practical relevance? And in particular, why would Christians have any interest in "vain philosophy" that the apostle Paul warns us against (Col. 2:8)?

The answer to that question is embedded in *The Devil Wears Prada,* the book that launched "chick lit," recently transformed into a (pretty decent!) film. In a key scene, Miranda (played so devilishly by Meryl Streep) is presiding over her entourage, trying to select just the right belt to accessorize the cover ensemble for next month's magazine. They are passionately deliberating between two belts which, to the untrained eye, look almost identical. Her fashion-averse assistant, Andy (played by Anne Hathaway), stumbles into the gathering. Growing impatient, and with a flippant disdain for fashion, she refers to the rack of designs merely as "stuff." Miranda, with that calm, satanic stare that Streep nailed so well, pauses, and quietly speaks to Andy:

"The Devil Reads Derrida: Fashion, French Philosophy, and Postmodernism," 850 Words of Relevant (Relevant Magazine Newsletter), October 23, 2006. Reprinted with permission.

Stuff? Oh, okay. I see. You think this has nothing to do with you. *You* go to *your* closet, and you select, I don't know, that lumpy blue sweater because you're trying to tell the world that you take yourself too seriously to care what you put on your back. But what you don't know is that sweater is not just blue. It's not turquoise. It's not lapis. It's actually cerulean. And you're also blithely unaware of the fact that in 2002 Oscar de la Renta did a collection of cerulean gowns. And then I think it was St. Laurent, wasn't it, who showed a selection of cerulean military jackets. And then cerulean quickly showed up in collections of eight different designers. It filtered down through the department stores, and then trickled down into some tragic Casual Corner where you undoubtedly fished it out of some clearance bin. However, that blue represents millions of dollars and countless jobs. It's sort of comical how you think you've made a choice that exempts you from the fashion industry, when in fact, you're wearing a sweater that was selected for you by the people in this room . . . from "a pile of stuff."

In this fabulous soliloquy in the middle of the film, Miranda articulates what we'll call the "trickle-down" theory of culture. Many spheres of cultural production, such as *haute couture* in the arcane parlors of Paris and Milan, seem to be merely the abstractions of the bourgeoisie — flights of fancy for the well-heeled who have the leisure for such play and silliness. But what does that have to do with *us,* down here, on the ground, schlepping to work on Monday mornings, or going to worship on Sunday mornings? Well, Miranda suggests, it has more to do with you than you might expect, because the fruits of these cultural labors in the upper echelons of French fashion eventually trickle down and impact what shows up on the racks at T. J. Maxx and Old Navy. While we might think we're immune from such worlds, in fact we are indebted to them all the time. The products of high-level fashion eventually filter down to the local strip mall and make an impact on how we all see ourselves (since fashion is such a crucial aspect of identity formation).

And what holds for French fashion holds true for French philosophy. The same "trickle down" principle is true, I'd argue, of the philosophical influence on culture. Now, I'm not really suggesting anything new here. In fact, this sense of the "trickle down" theory of culture animated the cultural engagement of Francis Schaeffer three generations ago. The idea is that, in important ways, current philosophical currents — which might seem arcane, abstract, and strange to those of us just trying to scrape together bus fare — have an impact on the shape of cultural practices. This is perhaps crystallized in discussions about "postmodernism." Phenomena often described as "postmodern" have a genealogy, and they track back to key shifts in philosophical thinking over the past half-century.

For instance, if we take the "emergent church" as something of a postmodern phenomenon, you will find that one of the key parts of that conversation involves questions of interpretation, authority, and meaning. Is there just one "right" interpretation? Can we know the author's intention when reading Scripture? Can some "authority" sanction the "one, true" interpretation of the Bible? Or are there multiple "true" interpretations? And could it be that *everything* is interpretation? If that's the case, what does that mean for the uniqueness of the gospel?

These are tough questions that tend to rattle the faithful. But these questions didn't just drop from the sky. In fact, they are questions that dominated twentieth-century European philosophy, particularly in the work of giants like Martin Heidegger and Jacques Derrida. And so it seems to me that if we're going to wrestle with tough questions, we also need to wrestle with the philosophical sources that put the questions on our plate.

So just as what shows up at T. J. Maxx has more to do with French fashion than we might think, so too what's discussed by the likes of Derrida and Foucault might be affecting our milieu more than we realize. If we are going to engage culture, and *make* culture, we will find it helpful to not just wait for things to trickle down, but to go looking for them at the source.

How might one do that? Well, reading would be a good start. If diving into Derrida or Foucault straight up seems daunting at first, I might recommend organizing a reading group around some introductions, such as my book, *Who's Afraid of Postmodernism?* (Baker Academic, 2006) or Crystal Downing's *How Postmodernism Serves (My) Faith* (IVP, 2006). For a more creative way into the conversation, invite some friends over and enjoy a couple of interesting documentaries available on DVD: *Derrida* (2002) and *Zizek!* (2005). Or consider listening in on the conversations at http://www.churchandpomo.org.

Chapter 26
OUR HISTORY OF VIOLENCE

A S YOU'D GUESS, David Cronenberg's film *A History of Violence*
interrogates violence on a number of different levels and includes
various modes of disturbance: from a sado-masochistic erotic
scene to violence against children, coupled with key scenes involving
bodily tissues and fluids. Cronenberg is clearly out to de-aestheticize
the violence that is a staple of Hollywood and, increasingly, our cultural
practices. He is trying to wake us up to what we might call, loosely para-
phrasing Hannah Arendt, the "banality of violence."

But the final sequence of the film is highly ambiguous, and so one
wonders what Cronenberg is after. Clearly, the closing scenes invite
theological reflection. The final sequence is launched by a Cain and Abel
encounter between brothers Joey Cusak (Mortensen) and Richie Cusak
(William Hurt)—invoking the "first violence" of Genesis 4. As Richie peers
up the barrel of Joey's pistol, he pleads, "Jesus, Joey. . . ." Joey responds
with a bullet to Richie's forehead, looks over his brother's body, and then
mutters under his breath, almost shaking his head: "Jesus, Richie. . . ."

We then cut to a scene of Joey at the lake behind Richie's mansion,
peeling off his blood-stained clothes (casting off the "old man" as it were),
and washing himself in the baptismal waters of the lake. He then makes
the long trip back from Philadelphia to his (now disrupted) ho-hum

"Our History of Violence," *Sightings,* published by the Martin Marty Center at the
University of Chicago, December 8, 2005; reprinted in *Circa: News from the University
of Chicago Divinity School* 25 (Spring 2006): 15. Reprinted with permission.

farmhouse in rural Indiana. Walking into his house, he finds his family (who know his history of violence) quietly eating at the table. In silence, the youngest daughter prepares a place for him at the table, inviting him to join the meal. His son Jack, who was enraged by his father's history of violence, passes him the meatloaf as an extension of hospitality, and his wife, Edie, simply looks at him through tears . . . and the celluloid goes dark. The film seems to end with Eucharistic hospitality, where the history of violence is forgiven when Joey is welcomed to the table.

But I think such a reading is taking Cronenberg's bait. In other words, I think Cronenberg is playing with us here, inviting us to see redemption where there is none. The utter ambiguity of the final scenes — including remarkably ambiguous expressions on the face of Joey and Edie — invites quite a different reading, one that is much more cynical. On this reading, Cronenberg is slyly inviting us to see our implication in violence, *our own* history of violence. (The use of the sex in the film is clearly intended to suck us into being erotically charged by violence, which is exactly what Hollywood [and Fox News] lives off of.) So on this alternative, decidedly un-Christian and perhaps even "pagan" reading (thinking of Milbank's discussion of the pagan in *Theology and Social Theory*), the first violence of Cain and Abel is a *necessary* violence, replayed over and over again, without end and without escape from the cycle. Joey's washing in the lake is not a redemptive cleansing, but more a matter of "washing one's hands," the wistful illusion of being done with violence, when in fact it is violence which nourishes all our practices and privileges. And his silent welcome to the table at home is not a matter of Eucharistic hospitality and forgiveness, but rather the silent complacency that wants to act "as if" we weren't implicated, "as if" the violence never happened, "as if" we can just get on with our lives and not talk about it. At the heart of this reading is a heightened sense of the banality of violence — that the pristine peace of every Mayberry is built upon a history of violence.

This second reading seems especially appropriate given recent revelations about the submerged violence that is quietly accepted as necessary for our "security." After all, isn't the price of sitting at the table of American security and prosperity the quiet acceptance of Abu Ghraib? Who are we to be aghast at the Cusak family's complicity when we live under the regime of an Attorney General who has defended the President's right to authorize practices that clearly violate the Geneva Convention? Aren't all of our dinner tables complicit with a system under which dozens have "disappeared" by "extraordinary rendition" to third countries where no one's watching?

This is why I think it is precisely this second, alternative reading of the film that would be the most "Christian." The real theological import of *A History of Violence* will be found in refusing the easy, almost trite, identification of Christian symbols and instead seeing in them a more sinister implication of us in our own histories of violence. In other words, I think Christians should read *A History of Violence* as a pagan comedy, not a Christian tragedy.

Chapter 27

HARRY POTTER AND
THE PROPHET OF DOOM

W HEN HARRY POTTER fans crack open *The Half-Blood Prince* (likely in the wee hours of Saturday morning), one of the things we'll be eager to learn relates to a prophecy revealed in the closing pages of *The Order of the Phoenix*. But the very notion of prophecy — as the foretelling of future events — would seem to compromise freedom. If Harry's future can be foretold, is he reduced to a kind of automaton, doomed to play out a sequence of events controlled by someone or something else? This is a tension long experienced by believers in a number of different religious traditions. J. K. Rowling has hinted at these questions throughout the chronicles of Harry Potter, but they crystallized in the conclusion to *Order of the Phoenix*.

THE HAUNTING PREDICTION ABOUT HARRY POTTER

Deep in the Department of Mysteries, Harry and his crew find a dusty glass orb which contains a prophecy given some sixteen years earlier. In the chaos of battle with the Death Eaters, the orb is shattered and the prophecy is released. But given all the commotion, no one can hear it, so only later does Dumbledore disclose the contents of the prophecy.

"Harry Potter and the Prophet of Doom," *Beliefnet.com,* July 15, 2005. Reprinted with permission.

It announces that "the one with the power to Vanquish the Dark Lord approaches" and would be born "as the seventh month dies" (sixteen years prior to this most recent disclosure — the year of Harry's birth). It further promises that "the Dark Lord will mark him as his equal . . . and either must die at the hand of the other for neither can live while the other survives."

The meaning of the prophecy seems quite clear. Even Dumbledore is convinced: the prophecy foretells a showdown between Voldemort and Harry. And Harry must be either murderer or victim.

But Harry's reaction is just what we would likely utter ourselves: Couldn't it be otherwise? Am I doomed to fate? How is that fair?

PROPHECY: MAGICAL VS. BIBLICAL

With these questions, J. K. Rowling explores terrain common in many religious traditions. Prophecy, providence, and predestination are especially central in the biblical traditions that have emerged from the Hebrew scriptures: Judaism, Christianity, and Islam. But how does prophecy in the magical world of Harry Potter compare with prophecy in the biblical tradition, particularly from a Christian perspective? The fulfillment of prophecy was crucial for the early church's proclamation. The Gospel accounts (especially the Gospel according to Matthew) are punctuated by claims that Jesus of Nazareth was the promised and prophesied Messiah.

While some of the philosophical questions about freedom and foreknowledge are the same, we might note several key differences between "magical" and biblical prophecy.

Consider the Source

Prophecy in the Bible is always surrounded by a good principle of journalism: *consider the source.* A false prediction compromised the integrity of the prophet and thus tainted everything that the prophet had to say.

If we apply this rule of discernment in the case of Harry Potter, we might wonder whether this isn't all much ado about nothing. After all, consider the source: the seer who made the prediction about Harry's mortal duel was none other than Madame Trelawney, introduced to us in *The Prisoner of Azkaban* as Hogwarts' resident quack — something Hermione quickly discerned. Trelawney regularly makes wrong predictions (especially concerning the annual student death count). Given her miserable track record, it's hard to know why Dumbledore seems so convinced that *this* prophecy (about Harry and Voldemort) is real. Her strange, trance-like voice seems to be a matter of importance. But even then, we need to consider the source: What if Trelawney's prophecy is akin to Harry's dream: a trap set by Voldemort? If Dumbledore operated with the biblical criterion of source suspicion, Trelawney's prediction should be disregarded.

A Matter of Interpretation

Madame Trelawney's predictions trade on ambiguity. The dregs of tea could be either a lump of mud, a bowler hat, or the dreaded Grim. It becomes a matter of interpretation, and it is just this hermeneutical ambiguity that feeds Hermione's empirical suspicions: "I think Divination seems very wooly," she remarks after their first class.

In biblical prophecy, there is also an element of ambiguity and interpretation. And here we have serious differences of interpretation. For instance, Christians read the prophecies of Isaiah 53 and see them fulfilled in Jesus of Nazareth. Jews are yet awaiting the fulfillment of that prophecy. The ambiguity of prophecy — whether magical or biblical — seems to come with the territory.

A God's-Eye Point of View

One question not yet tackled in Rowling's magical world is just *how* seers arrive at their predictions. By what mechanism or power do seers foretell the future? Here we run up against the crucial difference between magical and biblical prophecy. In biblical prophecy, the ultimate source of predictions is the God who transcends time: the Lord of history for whom all of time is present as a simultaneous "moment." Unlike human diviners somehow trying to stretch their sight into the future, for God the future is always present. Thus the Scriptures make a distinction between "soothsayers and diviners," who are to be rejected, and true "prophets," whose words are to be received as the Word of the Lord (Deut. 18:14-15).

It is this sense of transcendence that marks the difference between the worlds of Harry Potter and Jeremiah. Because there seems to be no transcendent standpoint in the universe created by Rowling, all prophecy is only divination.

THE FUTURE AND FREEDOM: FATE VS. PROVIDENCE

These differences noted, we are still left with questions about human freedom: Doesn't the notion of the future being predicted lead to a sense that we are not free? Does prophecy entail some sense of fatalism? How could we resolve these tensions, without giving up on prophecy and providence? Let me suggest one line of response.

Instead of thinking about discrete individual future *acts,* we should consider the future in terms of an *inevitability of character.* If I predict that tomorrow my wife will care for our children, I'm not discretely controlling the mechanism of her individual actions. Rather, I'm making a prediction based on the kind of person I know her to be: someone who loves our children. I'm counting on that, and I fully expect it to be fulfilled. But that does not compromise her "freedom." Predictions of this sort are rooted in the virtue or vice of the agents involved and take seriously their "agency" — a far cry from the common worry that prophecy reduces us to puppets of someone else's will.

PROPHETIC COUNSEL FOR HARRY POTTER

How might all of this help us to think about Harry's situation? Well, first, as suggested earlier, there might be good reason to reject Trelawney's prophecy as inauthentic. Harry and Dumbledore should carefully consider the source. Rejecting the prophecy would allow them the freedom to imagine the future otherwise. (Admittedly, this means that we, as readers, will have to reject the quasi-divinization of Dumbledore to which we're prone. But recall that Dumbledore confesses his certainty about this prophecy at the same time he recounts the many mistakes he's made about Harry's care. The wizard could be wrong. It remains to be seen whether Rowling agrees!)

But second, even if the prophecy is authentic, Harry need not feel as doomed as he does. If the prophecy foresees this battle of good vs. evil, this could be understood as an affirmation of Harry's character: that his confrontation with Voldemort is just what we would expect from someone with Harry's virtues. In that sense, Harry's agency is not threatened by predictions about his future actions. He is not simply a robot playing out someone else's will, but a virtuous agent whose commitments will inevitably lead to conflicts with the evil that threatens his world.

Of course, what really frightens Harry is the predicted result: that he will either kill or be killed. How are we to understand Harry's anguish about this? Does he despair about not being in control of his own future? Or does he despair at the thought of his own death? Is it the sense of inevitability that plunges Harry into despair? Or is this simply the fear of death?

At this point, I think Harry is less concerned with any metaphysical worries about prophecy and freedom, and more consumed with the question of death — and the after-life. As his closing attempts in *Order of the Phoenix* to make contact with Sirius indicate, while he might have been bothered by philosophical questions concerning predestination and freedom, he's now wrestling with theological questions about the after-life. Will *Half-Blood Prince* answer them?

Chapter 28

PASSING ON *THE PASSION*

AS A SPIRITUAL discipline for this Lenten season, I have a suggestion: resist the temptation to go see Mel Gibson's *The Passion of Christ*. If you take up this mode of Lenten denial, be prepared for strange looks. In the contemporary climate of the evangelical church, including here in Grand Rapids (where churches — including my own — are buying up entire viewings of the film and local pastors have lavished praise on the movie), your opposition to the film will be tantamount to sprouting a second head or remaining seated during the National Anthem. Despite being a minority position, I think there are good reasons for you to consider abstaining from the *Passion* craze.

First, the film raises an aesthetic and theological concern about the function of images of Christ. I should clarify at the outset: I am not an iconoclast. (I think Heidelberg Catechism Q/A 96-97 is a bit unfortunate but should be understood within a given historical context.) My reservations about *The Passion* do not stem from a principled opposition to images in general, or even images of Christ in particular. Along with a long iconic tradition in the holy, catholic church that we confess, I take it that the Incarnation underwrites an affirmation of images since Christ himself is the "image of the invisible God" (Col. 1:15).

However, on a theological and aesthetic level, it is precisely this iconic

---

"Don't just see Christ's body in 'The Passion,' instead be it," *Grand Rapids Press,* April 6, 2004. Reprinted with permission.

tradition that motivates my opposition to Gibson's *Passion*. Central to both the marketing of the movie and the reason people like James Dobson have endorsed it is what is described as the film's "disturbing realism." Gibson, a bit naively, has said that he wants to portray what it was "really" like for Christ to endure suffering for our sake. But the iconic tradition calls into question just these pretensions to "realism" and representation. Icons of Christ are intentionally *non*-representational; that is, they do not try to be "realistic," because the whole point of an icon is to be a window that points us "through" the painting to Christ himself. Paintings which try to be "realistic" tend to lose this "window-function," and we become absorbed with the reality of the work itself (think Caravaggio). But then it's no longer an icon: it's an idol. Because Gibson's film is so consumed with being "realistic," I think it has the character of an idol, not an icon.

Second, I think the fact that churches are latching onto *The Passion* as an evangelistic tool is a bit of a cop-out on the church's mission. In the New Testament, if people want to "see Jesus," even see the reality of his suffering, it is to be seen in his body — which is *us,* the church. I fear that the churches' evangelistic interest in the film as a way to *view* the suffering body of Christ is one more way of not having to *be* the body of Christ. Rather, you can take your neighbor to sit in a comfy cineplex and see the supposed "reality" of Jesus' sufferings — then hop in your SUV and go to Starbucks to talk about it. That's a bit strange, isn't it?

We are the ones who are sent, as the body of the ascended Christ, to be the light for the world — not the dancing light of the silver screen, or pretentious cinematic attempts to portray the "real" Jesus. Indeed, pinning our hopes on the light of the projected representations of Jesus might be just another way of avoiding our task of *being* the body of Christ, "in flesh and blood." Jesus wouldn't need to come to a "theater near you" if his body were bearing the light. Indeed, would the supposed "realism" of Christ's suffering in *The Passion* — viewed from the comfort of a suburban cineplex — be as compelling as seeing the *real* body of Christ — *us* — participate in the "fellowship of his sufferings" (Phil. 3:10)? According to Paul, if we the body were "always carrying about in the body the dying of Jesus" (2 Cor. 4:10), *then* the "life of Jesus [would] also be manifested in our body." If, instead of pursuing a life of middle-class comfort, we bore on our body the marks of Jesus (Gal. 6:17), wouldn't the supposed realism of a movie seem very distant and abstract?

Finally, we should be concerned about the commodification of the Passion. This hit home for me last week. While browsing in the periodical room of the Grand Rapids Main Library downtown, one of many magazines with a still from *The Passion* caught my eye. It was the cover of *CBA Marketplace,* the retail industry magazine of the Christian Booksellers Association. The theme of the cover article was "Reclaiming Easter," and it offered the following exhortation: "If it isn't about the Resurrection, what's it about? While Christmas may ring up cash registers, Christianity's greatest holiday celebration is Jesus Christ's resurrection — Easter. This year, converging activities and events offer potential for significantly increased evangelism, outreach, and store traffic. After seeing a preview of Mel Gibson's film *The Passion of the Christ* at CBA International Convention, CBA President Bill Anderson challenged Christian retailers and suppliers to be part of an industry effort to 'Reclaim Easter.'" In other words, this movie may help us to make Easter another season that makes cash registers sing. Those who claim to follow Christ, then, are urged to respond with an "industry effort" which could include the following strategies (included in "21 ideas to help maximize outreach, ministry, and sales"): strategically placing "special jewelry and prayer-card lines" just released by Bob Siemon designs, "develop a special 'this is what it's all about' slogan to position your store as the resource for Easter materials," and more. Churches have also joined in this commodification of the *Passion:* the narthex of our church included promotional flyers, door-knob hangers, postcards, and information about advance ticket purchases.

It's this very commodification of the film *by the church* that is disturbing to me, and it's not something that I want to participate in. In the vein of *The Prayer of Jabez* and *The Purpose-Driven Life,* here's one more marketing phenomenon generating a cottage industry of Christian consumer products (you just *know* that *The Passion* board games and Bible cases are on the way). As we approach this Lenten season, there's something that seems kind of disgusting about that. If we want to be imitators of the Crucified One, it seems to me that we bear witness by resisting such consumerism.

Chapter 29

FAITH IN THE FLESH IN *AMERICAN BEAUTY:* CHRISTIAN REFLECTIONS ON FILM

Grace makes beauty out of ugly things.

U2, "Grace," *All That You Can't Leave Behind*

LET ME GIVE you a little snippet of a conversation I've had several times over, usually at church — and once with my wife:

"You actually like American Beauty*?"*

"Like it?" I reply. "No, I love it. I think it might just be the one of the greatest films ever made. In fact, I show it every semester to my freshman philosophy class."

"You what*?" is the response, aghast. "Don't you teach at a* Christian *college? How could you expose your students to such a hopeless and filthy film?"*

"Well, I . . ." I'm interrupted.

"Is that the movie that opens with a man masturbating in the shower? And again later in the movie? And doesn't he try to sleep with a teenage girl? — his daughter's friend!"

"Well, yes, but . . ." It's no use: I'm interrupted again.

"Faith in the Flesh in *American Beauty:* Christian Reflections on Film," in *Imagination and Interpretation: Christian Perspectives,* ed. Hans Boersma (Vancouver: Regent College Publishing, 2005), pp. 179-89. Reprinted with permission.

"And isn't there a really pornographic scene of his wife's adulterous affair?"

"You seem to know the movie quite well," I quip — fleshly sarcasm getting the best of my Christian charity.

"And isn't, like, everybody and their brother gay in that movie? And doesn't the star of the movie smoke dope through the whole thing? And then end up getting shot in the back of the head in his own kitchen? That's the movie that you love — and you show that kind of a movie to freshmen at a Christian college?"

"I do," I assert, trying to stand tall. "It's a beautiful film. In fact, I think in some ways it's deeply Christian . . ."

That was too much: my interlocutor has already walked away, either for more coffee or to find the pastor.

American Beauty would seem to embody just about everything that Christians hate about Hollywood: profane language, graphic sexuality, adultery, homosexuality, drug content, child abuse, and more. It would seem to be a movie written as an illustration of what the New Testament describes as "the lust of the flesh" (Gal. 5:17; 1 John 2:16). Could we find a more carnal movie than *American Beauty*? Indeed, it would seem to be part of a cultural idolization of the sexual and erotic, symptomatic of a pagan culture "whose god is their belly" — or even a bit lower (Phil. 3:17; cp. Rom. 1:28-32). The generation of which *American Beauty* is a symbol is precisely a culture that puts its faith in the flesh.

But there is an interesting ambiguity about the flesh in the New Testament, isn't there? For as Christians, we also found our very confession and life on the fact that the "Word became flesh" (John 1:14). The Incarnation of God in Christ means that our relationship to *flesh* is more complicated and ambiguous.[1] I want to argue that if we really believe the Incarnation, then there is a deep sense in which we confess faith in the flesh: that the Lord is manifest in flesh, and that this should translate into an affirmation of the flesh. And if we are going to affirm the flesh in *this* sense — while

---

1. It should be noted here that, for Paul, *sarx* (the Greek word translated "flesh") does not refer to materiality *per se*, as if by "flesh" he meant "meat." But the play of the term in our own discourse makes this complicated.

still resisting "the flesh" in another sense — I think movies like *American Beauty* can open us up to such discipleship — a discipleship of the eyes, not just the mind.

I want to explore this theme on three levels: first, I want to invite you to put on your thinking caps with me for a few moments and indulge me in a little discussion of "metaphysics." We need to do this before we get to the good stuff: reflection on some central scenes in *American Beauty* which tell us something about the shape of a Christian film theory. Finally, I want to come back to some of the hard questions posed by my interlocutor at the beginning about what a discipleship of the eyes should mean for our movie-watching.

THE CHURCH, FILM, AND OUR ONTOLOGIES

I think the reason most Christians are suspicious of movies is *metaphysical,* not ethical. At stake in film theory is first of all an *ontology* (roughly, a philosophy of reality) which will determine how we understand the role of images (that is, the place of the *eikon*) vis-à-vis reality — an ancient philosophical question of the relationship between appearance and reality.

An ontology which I would describe as broadly "Platonic" tends to dominate Western thought (from Plato's *Republic* to Disney's *Beauty and the Beast* to the Wachowskis' *The Matrix*), concluding that images are dis-simulating, deceptive, and ultimately betray reality. This ontology begins from the assumption that what is "really real" (Plato's word) is the *im*material world which is invisible and cannot be sensed. The "sensible" or material world, according to this ontology, is at best a fallen copy of the real, immaterial world. Thus what is visible is *less real,* and in fact downright deceptive. So on this register there is a deep *dis*continuity between images and reality. The result is a consistent devaluing of the artistic and the production of iconoclasm in its many guises. One can see this in a fairly simple way in Disney's version of *Beauty and the Beast,* where things are not what they seem. Both Belle and the Beast must be schooled in seeing *through* and past appearances because, in the tradition of the (Platonic) cliché, appearances are deceiving. So while it *seems* that the Beast is a monster, the *reality* is otherwise. This dissimulative relation between appearance and reality is crystallized in the closing sequence of the film. Seizing a magical mirror that gives the villagers a glimpse of the Beast, his nemesis Gaston (a caricatured paragon of "manhood," and thus humanity) demonizes his monstrosity, whipping the village into a frenzy over the threat of a monster "who'll make off with your children." But Belle sees through all of this: "He's not the monster, Gaston," she exclaims. "You are!" So the one who appears monstrous is really the most humane, and the one who appears human is really the monster. There is thus a deep disconnection between appearance and reality, between "seeming" and "being."

This is the ontology which has generally captured the imagination of the Christian church (with some important Eastern exceptions). Reading the New Testament in a deeply Platonic manner, Christians have heard Paul's exhortations to "seek the things above" with Platonic ears, concluding that what's "really real" is not the material but the immaterial. What really matters is the *in*visible. The result has been a general *de*valuation of images and the artistic as distracting at best, deceptive and demonic at worst.

Opposed to this Platonic ontology is what we could describe as a "nihilist" ontology, which circumvents the question of the relation between appearance and reality by denying the distinction. Images are all we have, Baudrillard claims: there is no "original" behind them, only *simulacra* (as in Baudrillard, *Simulacra and Simulation* — the book in which Neo keeps his pirated software in *The Matrix*). This is a radically immanentist ontology which shuts down any reference to transcendence by denying the very distinction between immanent and transcendent, visible and invisible. It is this ontology which has increasingly captured what we might call "the postmodern mind." And in response, the church has often dug in its iconoclastic heels even more deeply. In other words, if the options are Nietzsche or Plato, we'll take Plato.

But to these alternative ontologies I want to oppose a third: an *incarnational* ontology which maintains the distinction between appearance and reality (contra Baudrillard), but also affirms the *continuity* between them (contra Plato). Hence, the image is not a dissimulation but rather a *revelation,* just as the Incarnation (the Word becoming flesh) was a genuine revelation of the invisible God. The development of an incar-national aesthetic (and film theory) is derived from two key biblical notions (prevalent, for instance, in Maximus the Confessor and John of Damascus): first, that Christ is "the image of the invisible God" (Col. 1:15), and second, that in the enfleshed Word the invisible God is made manifest (John 1:14, 18; 14:9). In the image, we do not have merely a copy but rather the "real presence" of the divine; thus, the iconic image is not a mere propaedeutic to later be discarded, but that which points to the transcendent and that in which the transcendent inheres. Thus an incarnational ontology affirms images in general, and film in particular, as a medium of *revelation.*

The ontology behind the Incarnation, which affirms materiality, is simply a *re*-affirmation of the goodness of creation. And it is *re*-affirmed again in the Christian hope of resurrection. Thus across the spectrum of the Scripture's narrative, we see a constant affirmation and re-affirmation of the goodness of materiality which runs counter to the Platonic *de*-val-uation of the material. But at the same time, this incarnational ontology also rejects the nihilist "flattening" of the world as if the material were all we had. Instead, an incarnational ontology affirms that there is *more* than the visible or material, and that this *in*visible "more" is what charges the material.

It is out of such an incarnational ontology that I think we can construct a Christian aesthetic more broadly, and a Christian film theory in particu-lar — what I will call a "revelational" or "revelatory" film theory.

A REVELATIONAL FILM THEORY IN *AMERICAN BEAUTY*

We can see the development of such a revelational film theory within a film, discerned in Ricky's "films" within the film *American Beauty.* Ricky's ongoing documentation of "beauty in the world" is in fact a quest for transcendence — a horizon opened by the lens of his camera, which offers him a perspective radically different from others. Thus the camera endues the filmed object with an iconic function or a sacramental value, reveal-ing transcendence — and "grace." We see this in several instances in the film, particularly in a central sequence beginning with Ricky's filming of a dead bird, moving to a discussion with Jane about death and his filming of a dead homeless woman, culminating in his presentation of "the most beautiful thing I've ever filmed."[2]

Ricky's account of beauty subverts both the Platonic and nihilistic ontology. Against Plato, he affirms the material as a positive medium for the revelation of transcendence. Against Baudrillard, he asserts that there is *more* than the material or visible, for these material phenomena function iconically as "windows" that open up to the transcendent — to something "behind" the material world. For instance, recalling his filming of a homeless woman who had died, Ricky comments: "When you see something like that, it's like God is looking right at you, just for a second. And if you're careful, you can look right back." But this revelation could only occur by means of the lens' sacralizing gaze, which both arrests and suspends the mundane.

This incarnational ontology is seen most clearly in Ricky's video of "the most beautiful thing [he's] ever filmed" (note that it is *filmed,* not simply "seen"): a plastic grocery bag dancing in the wind. Recounting the experience in almost mystical terms, he concludes: "That's the day I realized that there is an entire life behind things, and this incredibly benevolent force who wanted me to know there's no reason to be afraid. Ever." But again, the condition of possibility for this revelation and communication of grace is the sacramental gaze of the camera which makes the phenomenon "in the frame" revelatory; without it, it would be another piece of trash littering the street.

Other instances of the "sacralizing gaze" occur when Ricky films a dead bird in which he finds "beauty" and when Jane, earlier so consumed with the inadequacies of her body (we first meet her surfing the net, doing research on breast enhancement), exposes herself to the gaze of Ricky's lens, which — far from objectifying her — graces her with beauty.[3]

2. Actually, this sequence continues into a scene where Jane bears *herself* to the gaze of Ricky's lens, too.
3. When Ricky gazes at the face of Lester after the shooting, he too sees something there that others would not; however, this is not mediated by the lens of his camera, hence I don't include it above. The hint might be that eventually the camera's gaze can train the "bare" eye to see in the same way — again, a sort of discipleship of the eye.

The Camera as Sacrament:
Finding the Good in the Bad and the Ugly

So the camera both functions as a sacrament and bestows sacramentality: it is both a means of grace and the instrument by which "the world" is endued with grace. Through the lens and in the film, the world becomes *sacramentum mundi*. At stake here is an *ontology* which understands the structures of the world — even the most mundane, even the most "ugly" — as harboring a revelatory trajectory. This revelational capability inheres in the structure of the world.

At stake here is also a *phenomenology of perception:* whether the transcendence which inheres in creation is "seen" is a matter of perception, a matter for the perceiver — of which the camera is a model (both in the sense of being a "stand-in" and in the sense of being an exemplar). And yet it remains Ricky who sees through the camera; thus at issue is the subjectivity of the perceiver, the way in which he "constitutes" the world.[4] (At stake here would also be a hamartiology, a corresponding account of the way in which perception is "darkened" [Rom. 1:18-21] by sin. So I don't mean to suggest that film could be some sort of new "natural public theology.")

At stake here finally is a *liturgy;* insofar as the camera is a sacrament, the film becomes a medium for grace and revelation. The cinema becomes a sanctuary, if we have eyes to see. Or, to put it otherwise, the camera's gaze *trains* our own eye to see differently, so that eventually we can see the world the way Ricky's camera captures it: as a site of revelation. In this way, the cinema — where we view such films — is the site for a discipleship of the eye. It's important to see the role of community here: it is precisely the relationship with Ricky that makes it possible for Lester and Jane to see the world differently. This isn't something that they could have achieved on their own. They needed the catalyst of other co-viewers to learn to see *well*. (We should never watch movies alone.)

A revelatory art will also unveil the *brokenness* of the world for what it

4. This is another point of departure from Marion's phenomenology and why, ironically, I would argue that my incarnational aesthetic is closer to Deleuze's account of "immanence."

is: broken, fragmented, fallen, ugly, and violent. The world we inhabit isn't Eden or the *Little House on the Prairie*. So any work of art that is going to tell the truth about the world will have to tell it through the brokenness of a fallen creation. Here's where I think we come back to the problems posed by my interlocutor in our opening conversation. Obviously a film like *American Beauty* — and other great films such as *Magnolia* or Bergman's *Persona* — includes a lot of content and material that is not immediately "edifying." Christians especially tend to focus on the erotic and sexual aspects of the film.

But this Platonic or fundamentalist account is *not* a biblical understanding of the human person (that is, a flawed *ontology* gives us a flawed *anthropology*). When we begin from a theology that affirms the goodness of creation, that entails affirming the goodness of *bodies,* and all the aspects of embodiment associated with it — like dancing and sex. However, all of these "goods" of creation fit within a certain "order" of creation. Sexuality is part of the "grain" of the universe — a wonderful, important part of a good creation. And when this gift is received, welcomed, and celebrated *with* the grain of the universe, we will find wonder-full experiences of joy and shalom. But when the gift is *mis*-used — when we go against the grain — we will experience frustration, disappointment, and hurt. The "laws" of Scripture which some reject are in fact guardrails which are meant to guide us into the experience of joy and protect us from the pain of going against that grain. This is why John's first letter reminds us that God's commandments are not burdensome or oppressive (1 John 5:3).

Now this is precisely where I think the portrayal of sexuality in *American Beauty* stands in stark contrast to other films. Lester's erotic desire is, in the end, seen as a misplaced desire for authentic love and sexuality. When we meet him masturbating in the shower, the feeling that should be aroused is *sympathy:* "this," he tells us, "will be the highlight" of his day. It's part of a cycle of relational frustrations that characterize his isolated, individualistic suburban existence. Though his erotic desire is eventually directed towards Angela (Jane's teenage friend), in the end Lester discovers that this was — in Augustinian fashion — a misdirected desire (Freud would say a sublimated desire): all he really wants is Carolyn. When Angela, for just a moment, shows who she really is and declares her virginity, we, along with Lester, are to be aghast at the misdirection of our own desires. "This is my daughter!" we're led to say, along with Lester.

In short, the portrayals of sexuality in *American Beauty* are not gratuitous: in fact, they are calculated to unveil the very paucity of the erotic when it is misdirected (or "absolutized," Dooyeweerd might say). To put this in terms used above: the film shows what happens when sexuality runs *against* the grain of the universe (this is especially so in Carolyn's frustrated quest for intimacy with "the Real Estate King"). In this sense, it tells the truth about living in a fallen creation. This stands in stark contrast to the gratuitous inclusion of sex in many films, or the sanitized sitcom version of sexuality where sex "against the grain" goes on without consequence.[5]

If the arts — and film — are to be revelatory means of unveiling aspects of a broken creation, then we need to grant them the freedom to grapple with creation as we find it. So not only do I think Christians should *not* be concerned about a film like *American Beauty,* I think they should find elements of the gospel within it.

Does that mean that I think we can watch just anything? Couldn't someone come along and give a similar case, not for *American Beauty,* but for *American Pie?* What next: will someone be arguing that pornography shows us the sexual aspect of God's good creation? By no means! As I've just said: I think in works like these, we're dealing with lies because they don't show us the world as broken. Instead, they suggest that perverse sexuality or infidelity are normal, easy, and without disappointment, rather than something that is broken, heart-breaking, and runs "against the grain" of the universe.

But here I'm still capitulating to the evangelical fixation on sex and the erotic. I would be equally — perhaps more — concerned with violence in film. I know of youth groups which have shown *Braveheart* as modeling courage, and then encouraged their youth to go conquer the world for Jesus. But did anybody notice that the film is one of the most brazen presentations of violent revenge? If Christians are concerned about adultery,

---

5. See the excellent analysis on this score by Jenell Williams Paris, "The Truth about Sex," *Christianity Today,* November 12, 2001.

aren't we equally concerned with revenge? Or greed? Or pride? Before we start cataloguing films according to their sins, we should first go back to how un-critically we catalogue sins.

In fact, while *Focus on the Family* would direct our movie watching by counting the number of swear words or breasts that appear in a film, and though Christians are quick to condemn and reject a film like *American Beauty,* I think that the realm of "danger" in movie-going is somewhere completely different. In response to the question, "What kind of movies *shouldn't* we watch?" I would suggest just one word: *Disney.* Because what's more dangerous than the titillating temptations of *American Beauty* are the submerged idolatries of the Disney machine. Countless Christian homes immediately consider Disney films as "safe" viewing for their children (and I've been unsuccessful in convincing our children's grandparents otherwise). But the fact of the matter is that these films are bent on molding us into docile consumers in service of the god of mammon. *That,* it seems to be, is something to be worried about.

I believe in the flesh. That is, I confess that the Word was made flesh, and that God in Christ (in the flesh) was reconciling the world to himself. Because of that, I believe that the entire sphere of materiality and flesh is a site for the revelation of God's transcendence and an opening for the in-breaking of grace. If we follow through on that confession, I think we'll see the world the way Ricky does — even the ugly, broken aspects of the creation. Each will be a site for transfiguration. Film is a fleshy medium that can be understood incarnationally: the camera as a sacrament and the cinema as a sanctuary, operating in tandem to effect the discipleship of the eye.

Inspired by Encounters with Deleuze

Lord God,
Creator of earth and matter,
You both dazzle and hide,
You call both light and shadow to be.
You dwell on mountaintops
And in the nooks and crevices of the mountainside.
You speak in both fire and whispers.

Your very material creation —
With all of its dirt and blood,
All of its smells and tastes,
Is a playground for thought.

And so we — graced, privileged, and called — play
At what must seem to you, sometimes, just games.
Is God to be found in the trace? we ask, almost serious.
Is the world the folding and unfolding of God's immanence?
we inquire.
As we try out our questions, surely you chuckle, Lord —

Opening Prayer, Continental Philosophy Seminar, April 2003.

But I think that you chuckle because you like to play along —
That you are glorified in our play, even our serious academic play.

Only you, Lord, God of a richly folded creation,
Could be found in a place like Deleuze or Badiou,
Could surprise us in the pleats of French philosophers,
Could whisper in the creases of continental ontology.

Lord Jesus, you "sunk yourself in matter" for our sakes,
That we might be pulled out of our flat absorption in immanence —
To be the "charged" material image bearers of divine excess.
Help us, then, Lord, to be your disciples above all —
To discern what these texts mean for our discipleship,
For our being-in-the-world,
Our being-for-others,
And our being-before-you.
Amen.

INDEX OF NAMES

INDEX OF SUBJECTS